# The Telegraph
# Tax Guide 2025

# The Telegraph
# Tax Guide 2025

**Publisher's note**

Every possible effort has been made to ensure that the information contained in this book is accurate at the time of going to press, and the publishers and authors cannot accept responsibility for any errors or omissions, however caused. No responsibility for loss or damage occasioned to any person acting, or refraining from action, as a result of the material in this publication can be accepted by the editor, the publisher or the author.

First published as *The Daily Telegraph Guide to Income Tax* in 1974 by Constable & Robinson Ltd
This edition published in Great Britain and the United States in 2025 by Kogan Page Limited

All rights reserved. No part of this publication may be reproduced, stored or transmitted by any means without prior written permission from Kogan Page, except as permitted under applicable copyright laws.

**Kogan Page**

Kogan Page Ltd, 2nd Floor, 45 Gee Street, London EC1V 3RS, United Kingdom
Kogan Page Inc, 8 W 38th Street, Suite 902, New York, NY 10018, USA
www.koganpage.com

**EU Representative (GPSR)**

Authorised Rep Compliance Ltd, Ground Floor, 71 Baggot Street Lower, Dublin D02 P593, Ireland
www.arccompliance.com

Kogan Page books are printed on paper from sustainable forests.

© Telegraph Media Group, 2025

**ISBNs**

| Hardback | 978 1 3986 2222 7 |
| Paperback | 978 1 3986 2220 3 |
| Ebook | 978 1 3986 2221 0 |

**British Library Cataloguing-in-Publication Data**

A CIP record for this book is available from the British Library.

Typeset by Integra Software Services, Pondicherry
Print production managed by Jellyfish
Printed and bound by CPI Group (UK) Ltd, Croydon CR0 4YY

# CONTENTS

*About the author* xiii

**Introduction** 1

**01  You and HMRC** 3
Tax offices 3
Wealthy taxpayers 4
Taxpayers with particular needs 4
Accounts offices 4
Dealing with HMRC 5
Personal tax account 6
Compliance checks and enquiries 6
Determinations 7
Assessments and appeals 8
Prosecutions 8
Complaints 8
Changes in legislation 9

**02  Tax rates and allowances** 11
Income Tax rates 11
Scottish Income Tax rates 11
Allowances 12
Personal allowance 13
Marriage allowance 14
Married couple's allowance 15
Blind person's allowance 19

**03  Tax credits** 21
Child Tax Credit 21
Working Tax Credit 23
Tax credits and other benefits 24
Tapering 24
Annual renewal 24

## Contents

Changes in circumstances 25
Income disregard 26
Help and advice 26

**04 Interest payments and other outgoings** 27
Home annuity loans 28
Buy-to-let: finance costs 28
Business loans 30
Gift Aid 30
Gifts of assets to charities 32
Payroll giving 33

**05 Working in employment** 35
Am I employed? 35
Earnings 36
The Pay As You Earn (PAYE) system 36
Code numbers 36
Emergency tax codes 40
How tax is worked out using your tax code 41
Form P60 41
Starting work 43
Moving jobs 43
Tax-deductible expenses 44
Tax-free expenses 45
Employee travel 47
Home working 48
Benefits-in-kind 49
Employee share ownership 55
Enterprise Management Incentives 57
Payments on termination of employment 58

**06 Value Added Tax** 59
What is VAT? 59
Rates of VAT 59
Exempt supplies 60
Registration 60
Voluntary registration 62
Cancellation of registration 63

Help from HMRC  63
VAT invoices  63
Records, accounting and Returns  64
Online filing of Returns  65
Making VAT Digital  66
Input tax  66
Motor cars and fuel  67
Bad debts  68
Special schemes for retailers  69
Flat Rate Scheme  69
Cash accounting  70
Annual accounting  71
VAT visits and inspections  72
Penalties, surcharges and interest  72
Penalties if you pay late  74
Appeals  75
Complaints  75

## 07 Working for yourself  77
Am I self-employed?  77
Starting up in business  78
Records  78
Accounts  79
Cash accounting for businesses  83
Fixed-rate deduction scheme  83
Small business income allowance  84
Tax Return information  84
Profits for tax  86
Pre-trading and post-cessation expenses  87
Capital allowances  88
Losses  88
Limit of reliefs  90
Taking on staff  91
Some other ways to save on tax  91
Foster carers  92
Furnished holiday accommodation  93
Other special situations  94

## 08 National Insurance and state benefits 95
National Insurance numbers 95
National Insurance Contributions 96
Social Security benefits 98
Capital limits 102
Cap on benefits 103
Benefits and rates 104
State Pension Credit 104

## 09 State and private pensions 107
The new State Pension 107
Deferment 108
State Pension forecast 108
Private pensions 109

## 10 Savings and investment income 115
Tax-free income 115
Savings income 116
Dividend income 117
Accrued income 118
Rents 118
Rent-a-room 120
Non-qualifying life policies 121
Individual Savings Account 124
Lifetime ISA 126
Help-to-Save 126
Enterprise Investment Scheme 127
Seed Enterprise Investment Scheme 127
Venture Capital Trusts 128
Overseas investment income 128
Joint income 128

## 11 The family unit 131
Living together 131
Marriage/civil partnership 131
Children 132
High Income Child Benefit Charge 133

Tax-Free Childcare 134
The Child Trust Fund 134
Junior Individual Savings Account 135
Separation and divorce 135
Old age 136
Death 138

## 12 Residence and domicile 141
Residence 141
The automatic residence test 142
Sufficient ties test 142
Working abroad: expenses 144
Leaving the United Kingdom permanently 144
Allowances for non-UK residents 144
Income from UK property 145
Double taxation relief 146
Going abroad: Capital Gains Tax 146
Residential property in the United Kingdom 147
Coming to the United Kingdom permanently 148
Domicile 148
Changes in tax treatment of non-domiciliaries 149

## 13 Capital gains 151
Taxable gains 151
Tax payable 152
Married couples/civil partners 153
Working out chargeable gains 154
Relief for losses 155
Business Asset Disposal Relief 156
Investors' Relief 157
Assets owned on 31 March 1982 158
Investments in shares 158
Your home 159
Stamp Duty Land Tax 160
A second home 161
Chattels 162
Gifts and valuations 163
Short life assets 163
Part disposals 164

Enterprise Investment Scheme 164
SEIS 165
VCTs 165
Inheritances 166

## 14 How to complete your Tax Return and work out your tax 167

Do I need to complete a Tax Return? 167
Who has to complete a Tax Return? 167
Employees and pensioners with complex tax affairs 168
How do I register for Self Assessment? 168
Filing deadlines 169
The Tax Return 170
Getting started 171
Keeping proper records 171
Filling in your Tax Return 174
Working out your tax 183
Illustration 184
What HMRC do 186
Some other hints on efficient tax compliance 187

## 15 Paying your tax, interest and penalties 189

Tax payment dates 189
Payments on account 190
Reduced payments on account 190
Statements of Account 191
Paying your tax 192
Business Payment Support Service 194
What if I can't pay my tax? 194
Date of receipt 194
Interest 195
Remission of tax 196
Late payment penalty 196
Penalties 197

**16    Elections and claims: time limits** 201

**17    Inheritance Tax** 205
Rates of tax payable 205
Potentially exempt transfers 206
Chargeable lifetime gifts 206
Gifts with reservation and pre-owned assets 206
Exemptions 207
Your home 209
Business property 209
Agricultural property 210
Taper relief 210
Family home allowance 211
Transferable nil rate band 213
Death 215
Sales at a loss 217
Payment of tax 218
Interest and penalties 218
Excepted estates 219
Intestacy 219
Legacies 221
How to save on Inheritance Tax 221

**18    Budget measures** 223
Autumn Budget 2024 223

**Appendices** 225
1. Flat-rate allowances for special clothing and the upkeep of tools for 2024/25 225
2. HMRC (VAT) notices and leaflets 227
3. Rates of National Insurance Contributions for 2024/25 228
4. Social Security benefits 229
5. Rates of main Social Security benefits for 2024/25 230
6. HMRC (Revenue) explanatory booklets, leaflets and helpsheets 232
7. Main dates of the Self Assessment calendar: Saturday 6 April 2024 to Saturday 5 April 2025 234

*Index* 235

## ABOUT THE AUTHOR

Jon Yarker is an experienced financial journalist and copywriter. Since starting as a trade journalist at award-winning titles Citywire Wealth Manager and MoneyMarketing, he has established himself as a freelance journalist and regularly writes for various financial titles. He is IMC qualified.

# Introduction

We all want a better education for our children, an improved NHS, a more efficient and reliable transport system, less congestion on the roads and to feel safer and more secure in our homes and when we walk the streets. So who has to foot the bill for all these services? The government, of course. And how does the government raise the revenues to meet this expenditure? Mainly by taxing income, wealth, production and imports as well as collecting social contributions from us. Any deficit from one year to the next is funded by borrowing.

Several taxes and benefits are covered in this guide.

- Income Tax – what we pay annually on our earnings, pensions and income from savings.
- Capital Gains Tax – only paid when we realize profits on sales of some types of asset.
- Inheritance Tax – chargeable on some lifetime gifts of capital and on the value of our estates on death.
- Value Added Tax – included in the price of many goods and services we buy.
- National Insurance – the contributions we have to pay based on our earnings or business profits.
- Social Security – various benefits, including the State Pension, we may be able to claim.
- Tax credits – various sums that can be offset against a tax liability.

For many people tax is both confusing and complicated. This book aims to:

- explain the basics of the taxes covered for the average taxpayer as straightforwardly as possible;
- help readers have a better understanding of their tax affairs;
- make staying within the law as easy as possible; and
- help cut tax bills with pointers to saving on tax.

This edition of *The Telegraph Tax Guide* is primarily intended to cover the Self Assessment tax year from 6 April 2024 to 5 April 2025 and is being published soon after you need to submit a Tax Return for this year.

The tax changes announced by government in two fiscal statements in 2024 are set out in the final chapter of the book.

I hope you benefit from the read.

> Note that the HMRC forms in this book have been made as accurate as possible at the time of writing. Please visit GOV.UK for the most recent available HMRC forms.

# 01
# You and HMRC

First of all, you should have an understanding of the workings of the various HM Revenue & Customs (HMRC) departments responsible for the day-to-day running of our tax system.

The board of HMRC has overall authority for administering the fiscal legislation enacted by government. Although there are a large number of specialist departments within HMRC, it is likely that your only contact with it will be through the staff at your tax office and the accounts offices.

## Tax offices

Each tax office throughout the country is headed up by a senior officer with a full support staff. The tax affairs of employees and pensioners are looked after by the tax office that deals with the Pay As You Earn (PAYE) affairs of their employer or pension fund. If you are self-employed you may find that the tax office responsible for your tax affairs is sometimes local to your business address.

It is your service office that:

- sends you an email or letter telling you to complete a Tax Return;
- processes your Return when you send it back online or by post;
- corrects any obvious or simple errors that you have made and sends you a notice detailing the amendments; and
- initially chases you up if you are late submitting your Return.

Service offices are also responsible for:

- looking after all the day-to-day tax matters of the vast majority of taxpayers whose income is taxed under PAYE and who do not come within the system of Self Assessment; and
- processing the business accounts of self-employed taxpayers.

As long as you comply with all your tax obligations in a timely manner, your only involvement with HMRC will be confined to your service office.

## Wealthy taxpayers

If you are one of the wealthiest taxpayers, your tax affairs are looked after by one of the HMRC High Net Worth Units (HNWU). It is intended that each HNWU will:

- build relationships to help better understand these taxpayers and make it easier for them to get things right; and
- better tailor service delivery for these taxpayers through proactive engagement and by providing a single point of contact as well as a holistic approach for their tax affairs.

## Taxpayers with particular needs

HMRC offer a range of facilities for taxpayers with particular needs; for example, if:

- you are blind or partially sighted;
- you are deaf, have impaired hearing or have a speech impediment; or
- your first language is not English.

If you think you need extra help, the number to call is 0300 200 3300. Those calling from outside the UK should call +(44) 135 535 9022.

## Accounts offices

The main tasks of HMRC accounts offices are to:

- bank payments of tax and National Insurance Contributions; and
- keep up-to-date, accurate payments records.

If you need to telephone, write to or visit any of these offices, always give your name and reference number. You can find the address and telephone number on forms and letters that have been sent to you.

# Dealing with HMRC

Information about the following is available to you by telephoning 0300 200 3300:

- changes in your personal circumstances;
- employment details;
- claims to personal allowances;
- employee benefits;
- savings and investment income;
- State and other pensions;
- taxable State benefits;
- income from renting out your home when you are away;
- other property income;
- making amendments to your Self Assessment Return;
- dealing with tax repayments due to you.

In most cases nothing more will be needed from you, although the call may lead to further action by HMRC (for example, sending out a revised PAYE Coding Notice). Where your business cannot be completely dealt with by telephone, the HMRC officer will arrange to send you any necessary forms or follow-up material.

On any matter that does not come within the 'business by telephone' services, you can put any questions in writing to HMRC at: Pay as You Earn and Self Assessment, HM Revenue & Customs, BX9 1AS.

Whenever you telephone or write, always remember to quote your reference number, which is:

- your employer's PAYE reference; or
- your National Insurance number; or
- if you are self-employed or pay tax at the higher rate, your Self Assessment Unique Taxpayer Reference (UTR), a 10-digit number.

## Personal tax account

By setting up a personal account, you can check your records and manage tax affairs with HMRC.

This can enable you to handle your tax affairs online, promptly and simply, whenever you choose to do so.

Furthermore, it is secure, personalized and assembles all your tax matters in one place.

To sign in you will need a Government Gateway account (which you will have if you have already used HMRC online services) and your National Insurance number.

Once you have signed in you can use your personal tax account for a range of services, for example to:

- complete, send and view your annual Tax Return;
- check your Income Tax estimate and tax code;
- claim a tax repayment;
- tell HMRC when you move home;
- check and manage any tax credits that you receive; and
- find out about your State Pension.

This is just a snapshot of what you can do. HMRC intend that more services will be added at a later date.

## Compliance checks and enquiries

Once your Return has been processed by your tax office, it will undergo a comprehensive programme of checks. Any obvious errors, for example in your arithmetic, will be corrected. Alternatively, HMRC will write or telephone to resolve any other queries relating to:

- your Self Assessment Tax Return;
- your accounts and tax calculations; and
- the taxes you pay.

In most cases, no further questions will be asked. But enquiries will be started by your tax office if:

- something requires fuller explanation;
- there is a risk your Return may be incorrect; or
- your Return is selected for enquiry at random.

Normally, HMRC have 12 months from the date that your Return is received by your tax office in which to tell you that it will be the subject of enquiries.

Your Return will normally become final if your tax office has not raised any enquiries within the permitted time period. HMRC can only raise enquiries at a later date if they discover an error that they could not reasonably have been expected to be aware of from the information provided in, or with, your Return.

At the end of an enquiry into your Return, HMRC will issue a closure notice, which will include the making of any necessary adjustments to your Self Assessment. You have 30 days in which to appeal against such amendments.

Any enquiries by your tax office should be conducted in accordance with the specific code of practice laid down by HMRC. If your Tax Return ever becomes the subject of an enquiry, this may well be a time when you should be represented by a professional tax adviser.

## Determinations

Not surprisingly, HMRC has special powers to deal with taxpayers who are sent a Return but fail to complete it and submit it by the filing date. In such cases an offending taxpayer can expect HMRC to make a determination of his or her income and capital gains chargeable to tax to the best of their knowledge and belief. The actual amount of tax is based on estimates of:

- the taxpayer's allowances and reliefs; and
- tax deducted at source on earnings and savings income.

Any determination can be subsequently superseded by:

- a Self Assessment by the taxpayer; or
- HMRC based on information provided by the taxpayer.

## Assessments and appeals

In cases of fraud or neglect, your Tax Inspector can raise an assessment to collect tax that should have been paid on a Self Assessment. You do, of course, have a right of appeal against:

- an assessment raised by your Tax Inspector; or
- an amendment to your Return following an enquiry.

The procedure for resolving your appeal starts with a hearing before an independent tribunal of expert tax judges and/or panel members. It can then move on to the courts and ultimately to the Supreme Court.

## Prosecutions

An important role of HMRC is to deter fraud. They will prosecute in serious cases in all areas of the tax system. Cases selected for prosecution involve a wide range of offences. However, a case is more likely to be considered for prosecution if it contains features such as:

- falsification of documents;
- lying during an investigation; or
- discovery of false documents made during an earlier investigation.

## Complaints

Any complaint should, first of all, be made to the tax office with which you are dealing, either by telephone, in writing or online. Address your letter to the Officer in Charge. You should explain:

- the complaint (for example, slow service, constant mistakes);
- when it happened;
- who dealt with you;
- what effect HMRC's actions had on you; and
- how you would like HMRC to resolve the problem.

Most complaints about HMRC's handling of people's tax affairs are satisfactorily settled by their tax office. Where taxpayers are not satisfied with the response from their office, they can take their case to a different complaints handler.

Taxpayers who are still dissatisfied can put their case to the HMRC Adjudicator, who will review all the facts and try to reach a decision as soon as possible. HMRC normally accept this decision unless there are exceptional circumstances.

Taxpayers can also ask a Member of Parliament to refer their complaint to the Parliamentary and Health Service Ombudsman. The Ombudsman, which is independent, will look into a complaint, but usually after it has first of all been considered by the Adjudicator.

# Changes in legislation

The Chancellor of the Exchequer usually makes an annual Budget Statement in the spring and Autumn Statement in October or November. Traditionally the Budget focuses on taxation for the next year while the Autumn Statement tends to be about economic projections and how much government departments will have to spend. However, that distinction has become increasingly blurred in recent years.

After the Chancellor has announced their tax plans in the Budget the resulting legislative changes are published in the Finance Bill. Its various clauses are debated by Parliament and occasionally amended. Subsequently, the Bill is passed by both Houses of Parliament before receiving Royal Assent. It is then published as a Finance Act.

When the law is either unclear or ambiguous, HMRC will issue a Statement of Practice indicating how they intend to interpret it. There are also times when HMRC do not seek to go by the strict letter of the law. These are gathered together and published as a list of Extra-Statutory Concessions.

# 02
# Tax rates and allowances

For most of us our annual tax bill is determined by tax bands, rates and the allowances we can claim.

## Income Tax rates

Under our tax system, the tax (or fiscal) year runs from each 6 April to the following 5 April. The rates of tax for 2024/2025 are:

| Band of taxable income (£) | Rate of tax (%) | Tax on band (£) | Cumulative tax (£) |
|---|---|---|---|
| 0–12,570 | 0 | | |
| 12,571–50,270 | 20 | 7,540 | 7,540 |
| 50,271–£125,140 | 40 | 34,976 | 42,516 |
| Over 125,141 | 45 | | |

The rates of 20 per cent and 40 per cent are respectively known as the basic and higher rates. The additional rate refers to tax at the 45 per cent level.

There are special rules and rates for working out the tax you pay on your savings and dividend incomes (see Chapter 10).

## Scottish Income Tax rates

You will pay Scottish Income Tax if your main home is in Scotland, or you move to Scotland and live there for over half the tax year.

The rates of tax for 2024/25 are:

| Band of taxable income (£) | Rate of tax (%) |
|---|---|
| 12,570 to 14,876 | 19 |
| 14,877 to 26,561 | 20 |
| 26,562 to 43,662 | 21 |
| 43,663 to 75,000 | 42 |
| 75,001 to 125,140 | 45 |
| Over 125,141 | 48 |

Scottish Income Tax is payable on your wages, pension and most other taxable income. But you pay the same tax as the rest of the UK on your savings income and dividends.

## Allowances

The rates of the various tax allowances for 2024/25 are:

| | £ |
|---|---|
| **Personal** | |
| All individuals | 12,570* |
| **Married couples** | |
| Either spouse/partner born before 6 April 1935 | 11,080**/*** |
| Minimum amount | 4,280*** |
| **Marriage** | |
| Transferable marriage allowance | 1,260 **** |
| **Relief for blind person (each)** | 3,070 |

\* The personal allowance reduces at the rate of £1 for every £2 of income in excess of £100,000.

\*\* The married couple's allowance comes down by £1 for every £2 of income above a specified limit – £34,600 for 2024/25.

\*\*\* Indicates allowances where tax relief is restricted to 10 per cent.

\*\*\*\* Available to spouses/civil partners born after 5 April 1935.

In working out the amount of Income Tax payable each year:

- the personal, blind person's and transferred marriage allowances are taken off total income; and
- tax relief for the married couple's allowance is given as a deduction from tax payable.

# Personal allowance

Every man, woman or child, single or married and resident in the United Kingdom, can claim the personal allowance. This is set against total taxable income from all sources, such as:

- a wage, salary or business profits;
- an occupational and/or a State Pension;
- interest on savings;
- income from investments; and
- rental income.

The personal allowance reduces at the rate of £1 for every £2 of income in excess of £100,000.

---

During 2024/25 Richard West, a married man in his early 40s, earned £36,500 from his job. His tax liability for the year is £4,786, worked out as follows:

|  | £ |
|---|---|
| Salary | 36,500 |
| *Less*: Personal allowance | 12,570 |
| Taxable income | 23,930 |
| Income Tax payable |  |
| £23,930 @ 20 per cent | 4,786 |

> Paul Frost received remuneration, including benefits, of £110,000 during 2024/25. His tax liability for the year amounted to £33,432, worked out as follows:
>
> |  | £ |
> |---|---|
> | Remuneration | 110,000 |
> | *Less*: Personal allowance | 7,570 |
> | Taxable income | 102,430 |
>
> |  | £ |
> |---|---|
> | Income Tax payable | |
> | £37,700 @ 20 per cent | 7,540 |
> | £64,730 @ 40 per cent | 25,892 |
> |  | 33,432 |
>
> Your Personal Allowance goes down by £1 for every £2 that your adjusted net income is above £100,000. Therefore, Paul's personal allowance for the year is reduced by £5,000 being 1/2 x (£110,000 – £100,000) from £12,570 to £7,570.

## Marriage allowance

You can claim the marriage allowance if all of the following requirements apply.

- You are married or in a civil partnership.
- Both of you were born on or after 6 April 1935.
- Your income for 2024/25 is not more than £12,570, plus up to £5,000* of savings income.
- Your spouse or partner's income for 2024/25 is between £12,571 and £50,270.

*After taking off your Personal Savings Allowance.

> **Tax Saver**
>
> The marriage allowance enables you to transfer £1,260 of your 2024/25 personal allowance to your spouse or partner. By so doing you will save tax of £252 (£1,260 @ 20 per cent).

Clearly it is only advantageous to claim the marriage allowance in cases where one spouse or civil partner is unable to claim all or part of their personal allowance because of a low income.

You can apply for the marriage allowance by registering online at www.gov.uk/apply-marriage-allowance. If your application is accepted, the changes to your own and your spouse's/partner's personal allowances will be backdated to the beginning of the tax year.

If you or your spouse/partner were born before 6 April 1935 you may be able to claim the married couple's allowance (see below).

Other features of this measure are the allowance is transferable in full or not at all, and will always be equivalent to 10 per cent of the rounded-up personal allowance.

# Married couple's allowance

You can claim the married couple's allowance if you can satisfy all of the following.

- You are married or in a civil partnership.
- One of you was born before 6 April 1935.
- You are living together.

It is the husband's income which is used to calculate the married couple's allowance for a couple married before 5 December 2005. For marriage and civil partnerships after this date it is the person with the higher income.

> **Tax Saver**
>
> For 2024/25 the married couple's allowance could lower your tax bill by anywhere between £427 and £1,108 a year.

> **Tax Saver**
>
> For some reason you may not be able to live with your spouse or civil partner. This may be because:
>
> - a spouse or partner needs to be in residential care owing to illness or old age;
> - your job takes you away from home;
> - you are in education or training; or
> - you are in prison.
>
> When you are living apart through any of these circumstances you can still claim the married couple's allowance.

> Eric Black was 88 years old in 2024/25. His younger wife, Myra, celebrated her 68th birthday the same year. They are entitled to allowances of £23,650 and £12,570 as follows:
>
> |  | Eric (£) | Myra (£) |
> | --- | --- | --- |
> | Personal allowance | 12,570 | 12,570 |
> | Married couple's allowance | 11,080 |  |
> | Total allowances | £23,650 | 12,570 |

> Long-standing partners Rex Gardner and Gerald Sullivan entered into a civil partnership on 4 January 2016. They are both in their late-80s. Gerald, who has the higher income, can claim the married couple's allowance of £11,080 for 2024/25.

## Tax rates and allowances

The amount of the married couple's allowance in the year of marriage:

- depends upon the time in the year that the wedding takes place; and
- is reduced by one-twelfth for every complete month from 6 April up to the day of the marriage.

---

Percy Hughes, aged 87, married his wife, Barbara, aged 73, on 10 November 2024. He receives an allowance of **£4,617** for 2024/25, worked out as follows:

|  | £ |
|---|---|
| Married couple's allowance | 11,080 |
| *Less*: Reduction |  |
| 7/12 × £11,080 | 6,463 |
| 2024/25 allowance | 4,617 |

---

There is no reduction in the married couple's allowance for a year when:

- couples separate;
- couples divorce; or
- one spouse dies (a widow is entitled to any unused part of the married couple's allowance for the year in which she loses her husband).

---

### Tax Saver

If you cannot benefit from the full amount of the married couple's allowance because:

- you are not a taxpayer; or
- your tax bill is not big enough,

you can transfer the balance to your spouse or partner by completing form 575(T).

---

A wife does not need her husband's consent to claim one half of the minimum amount of the married couple's allowance, £2,140 for 2024/25. Alternatively, a married couple can jointly elect for the wife to receive the full minimum amount of the allowance, £4,280 for 2024/25. Such an election:

- must be made using HMRC Form 18;

- must normally be made before the start of the tax year for which it is to apply (except in the year of marriage, when the newlyweds can submit a notice dealing with the reduced married couple's allowance for that year); and
- once made carries on from year to year until changed by the couple.

---

James Lucas, who is in his late-80s, had income from pensions of £14,000 in 2024/25. His wife, Mary, who is 20 years younger than James, is still working and earned a salary of £15,500 in 2024/25. She elected to receive one half of the basic married couple's allowance. James does not pay any tax for 2024/25 as follows:

|  | £ |
| --- | --- |
| Pensions | 14,000 |
| *Less*: Personal allowance | 12,570 |
| Taxable income | 1,430 |
| Income Tax payable |  |
| £1,430 @ 20 per cent | 286 |
| *Less*: Relief for married couple's allowance £11,080 − (1/2 × £4,280) = £8,940 @ 10 per cent | 894 |

Mary has a tax bill for the year of £372 as follows:

|  | £ |
| --- | --- |
| Salary | 15,500 |
| *Less*: Personal allowance | 12,570 |
| Taxable income | 2,930 |
| Income Tax payable |  |
| 2,930 @ 20 per cent | 586 |
| *Less*: Relief for married couple's allowance £2,140 (1/2 × £4,280) @ 10 per cent | 214 |
|  | 372 |

---

The purpose of the married couple's allowance is to assist elderly taxpayers on low and modest incomes. It follows, therefore, that this allowance is restricted when total income, after permitted reliefs and deductions, exceeds a specified limit – £37,000 in 2024/25. The reduction is £1 for each £2 by which total income is more than the annual stated limit.

However, there is a minimum amount of £4,280 for the married couple's allowance.

# Blind person's allowance

This allowance is given to a registered blind person. Where both husband or wife or civil partners are blind or have severely impaired sight, each of them can claim the allowance.

If either of them is on a low income and unable to use up his or her allowance, any unused part can be transferred to the other even if he or she is not blind. The allowance for 2024/25 is £3,070.

When a taxpayer first becomes entitled to this special allowance, by being registered blind, the allowance will also be given for the previous tax year if, at the time, the individual had received the necessary proof of blindness needed to qualify for registration. This concession prevents individuals losing out as a result of any delays in the registration process.

The allowance is not available to registered partially sighted individuals.

# 03
# Tax credits

If you are on a low or modest income, you may already be claiming one of two tax credits: Child Tax Credit or Working Tax Credit.

- Child Tax Credit (CTC) is paid to individuals who are responsible for children. It does not matter whether claimants do, or do not, work.
- Working Tax Credit (WTC) is paid to those in work and is targeted at low wage earners and workers who use formal childcare.

However, these credits, and several other benefits, are being replaced by Universal Credit. Many existing claimants have already been moved over to Universal Credit and that process should complete in 2025.

If you're a new claimant and you need support you should apply for Universal Credit. We discuss Universal Credit in more detail in Chapter 8.

## Child Tax Credit

CTC is:

- paid to some individuals responsible for at least one child or qualifying young person; and
- paid by direct transfer to the bank account of the person (usually the mother) mainly responsible for the care of the child or children.

A child is a person under 16 years old or, in the case of a 16-year-old teenager, until 31 August after their 16th birthday.

A qualifying young person is someone who is:

- no longer a child;
- under 20 years old; and
- in full-time education; or
- on an approved training course.

You are usually responsible for a child if:

- they live with you permanently;
- you are their main carer and they normally live with you;
- their toys and clothes are kept in your home; or
- you feed them and give them spending money.

If you share responsibility for a child and you cannot reach agreement on which of you claims, you can both apply. In this situation the Tax Credit Office will make the decision.

CTC is made up of the following elements:

| Rates for 2024/25 | Annual (£) |
|---|---|
| Family element | 545 |
| Child element (each child) | 3,455 |
| Disabled child element* | 4,170 |
| Severely disabled child element** | 1,680 |

*In addition to the child element.
**As well as the child and disabled child elements.

What you get depends on:

- whether you are already receiving CTC; and
- the date when your claim started.

| Elements of CTC | Date claim started | |
|---|---|---|
|  | Before 6 April 2017 | On or after 6 April 2017 |
| Family element | Yes | Only if one child was born before 6 April 2017 |
| Child element | All children born before 6 April 2017* | Up to two children only |

* You will only get the child element for a baby born after 6 April 2017 if the baby is your second child.

# Working Tax Credit

Existing claimants for WTC must be:

- between 16 and 24 years old, have a child or be disabled; or
- aged 25 or over, with or without children.

You have to work a specific number of hours in a week to receive WTC as follows.

| Your situation | Working hours per week |
| --- | --- |
| Age 25–59 | 30 hours minimum |
| Over 60 years old | 16 hours minimum |
| Disabled | 16 hours minimum |
| Single with at least one child | 16 hours minimum |
| Couple with one or more children | Normally at least 24 hours between them – one has to work for at least 16 hours |

There are special rules for some couples:

- with at least one child; and
- who work for less than 24 hours a week between them.

The childcare element of WTC is paid, with entitlement to WTC, to the person responsible for the care of the child or children. WTC comprises the following elements.

| Rates for 2024/25 | Annual (£) |
| --- | --- |
| Basic entitlement | 2,435 |
| Additional couples, and lone parent, element | 2,500 |
| 30-hour element | 1,015 |
| Disability element | 3,935 |
| Severe disability element | 1,705 |
| Childcare element | |
| • maximum eligible cost | 300 |
| • maximum eligible cost for one child | 175 |
| Percentage of eligible cost covered | 70% |

## Tax credits and other benefits

If you receive tax credits, you may get less:

- income-based Jobseeker's Allowance
- Income Support
- income-related Employment and Support Allowance
- Housing Benefit; or
- State Pension Credit.

The office that deals with the payment of your benefits will be able to work out how these are affected by tax credits.

## Tapering

Tax credits taper away at a rate of 41 per cent for each £1 of family income over a threshold of £7,955 (£19,995, where no WTC is claimed). The first £300 of income from pensions, savings and property is excluded. The order of reduction is:

- WTC;
- childcare element of WTC;
- child elements of CTC; and
- family element of CTC.

> ### Tax Saver
>
> For taxpayers claiming tax credits and paying pension contributions, not only will they see their tax bill come down but they may also qualify for an increase in their tax credits award as pension contributions reduce income for tax credit purposes.

## Annual renewal

Every year between April and June each existing claimant will receive a renewal pack that serves two purposes:

- first, to establish actual income for the year just ended and to check on the claimant's circumstances; and
- second, to make the claim for the new year.

You have until 31 July to complete and return the forms. Once the information you have provided has been processed, you will receive a notice about your final tax credit for the year recently ended.

If you have received too much tax credit you will be expected to refund the excess. This will usually be done by restricting the reward for the year following.

If you have been paid too little tax credit you will receive the extra amount as a single payment.

## Changes in circumstances

Once a claimant has been granted tax credits, even for a nil amount, he or she has a duty to advise HMRC online, or by post or telephone, within 30 days of certain stipulated changes in circumstances. These are:

- marriage, moving in to live with a partner or entering a civil partnership;
- divorce, separation from, or death of, a partner;
- a child or partner dies;
- a child over 16 leaves either education, training or a careers service;
- a child moves out, goes into care or is taken into custody;
- a drop of more than £10 a week in the average costs of childcare;
- discontinuing payment to a childcare provider;
- childcare provider ceases to be registered or approved;
- working hours falling below 30 a week (16 if you are claiming childcare costs);
- working hours falling below, or going above, the minimum required to qualify;
- going abroad for at least eight weeks; and/or
- leaving the United Kingdom permanently.

You should also notify HMRC as soon as you can of other changes, which include:

- the birth of a child;
- change of address, bank details or childcare provider;
- you start paying for, or stop getting help with, the costs of approved childcare;
- you begin claiming benefits or any of your existing benefits change;
- a child is certified blind;
- someone in the household becomes disabled; or
- a change to your working hours from under 30 a week to 30 or more.

## Income disregard

Not only is a claimant's entitlement to tax credits continuously adjusted by alterations in lifestyle circumstances but it is also affected by changes to income in the award period, namely a tax year.

When a claimant's income drops, a higher award can be immediately requested. However, a drop in income of up to £2,500 in a claim year is disregarded in assessing any increase in entitlement.

Conversely, when income increases the amount of the award will come down. However, a claimant's income for tax credit purposes can increase by as much as £2,500 in a claim year, compared to the previous year, without any reduction in entitlement. This gives more certainty to claimants that their payments will not suddenly be decreased when their income goes up during an award period.

Any change in annual income of £2,500 or more, up or down, must be reported immediately.

## Help and advice

If you would like help or advice about tax credits, there are several sources to turn to.

- Phone the Helpline on 0345 300 3900 (England, Scotland and Wales) or 0345 603 2000 (Northern Ireland).
- Go online to www.gov.uk/taxcredits.
- Visit a local advice service such as a Citizens Advice Bureau who may be able to help.

# 04
# Interest payments and other outgoings

The opportunities for claiming tax relief on interest paid on borrowings are few and far between. These include the following.

- The purchase, in certain circumstances, of life annuities if you are aged 65 or over.
- Buying a share in:
  - an employee-controlled company;
  - a close company (ie controlled by five or fewer shareholders), or lending capital to it;
  - a partnership, or contributing capital to a partnership, if you are a partner.
- Buying plant and machinery for use in your job or partnership so long as the plant and machinery attracts capital allowances for tax purposes (see Chapter 7).

Interest is also allowable for tax purposes on a replacement loan where the interest on existing borrowings qualifies for tax relief.

It is important to understand that the purpose for which a loan is advanced governs whether the interest on it will be eligible for tax relief. How the loan is secured is not relevant.

Other than interest paid on a loan taken out to acquire buy-to-let property, the interest on which tax relief is due is deducted from your total income in the year of payment. It cannot be spread over the period of accrual, nor can tax relief be claimed if the interest is not actually paid.

> **Tax Saver**
>
> As you do not get tax relief on mortgage interest to buy your own home, it might be worthwhile using any spare cash on deposit with a bank or building society to repay some or all of your mortgage.

## Home annuity loans

This is a form of relief that is not available to many people and has previously come close to being abolished by the government. Nevertheless, it's worthwhile we cover it.

Interest on a loan taken out before 9 March 1999 to purchase an annuity (an investment providing a fixed or increasing annual sum) from an insurance company still attracts tax relief at 23 per cent provided:

- the borrower was at least 65 years old at the time the annuity was purchased;
- not less than 90 per cent of the loan on which the interest is payable went towards buying an annuity for life; or
- security for the loan is the borrower's main residence.

The maximum loan on which tax relief is allowed is £30,000. Where a loan exceeds this limit, tax relief is given on the proportion of the total interest payable equivalent to the £30,000 limit. Income Tax at the special rate of 23 per cent will be deducted at source by the insurance company in working out the regular payments to be made by the borrower.

## Buy-to-let: finance costs

Tax relief on finance costs such as interest on:

- mortgages;
- overdrafts; and
- loans, including those to purchase furnishings,

is restricted for individuals who receive rental income from letting residential property both in the UK and overseas.

From the 2020/21 tax year onwards, these individuals have been prohibited from deducting mortgage expenses from their rental income. Instead, they receive a tax credit based on 20 per cent of their mortgage interest payments.

---

Ryan Morgan received a salary of £45,000 from his employer in 2024/25. His rental income, after allowable expenses, was £12,000 in the same year. He paid mortgage interest of £9,000 on loans taken out to acquire his let properties. His tax liability for the year is £9,592, calculated as follows:

|  | £ | £ |
|---|---|---|
| Salary |  | 45,000 |
| Net rental income | 12,000 |  |
|  |  | 57,000 |
| Less: Personal Allowance |  | 12,570 |
| Taxable income |  | 44,430 |
| Less: tax credit (£9,000 × 20%) |  | 1,800 |
| Taxable income |  | 42,630 |
| Income Tax payable |  |  |
| £37,700 @ 20 per cent |  | 7,540 |
| £5,130 @ 40 per cent |  | 2,052 |
|  |  | 9,592 |

Additionally, Ryan can increase the loan up to the original cost of the property and obtain 20 per cent tax relief.

---

Any finance costs which:

- you have incurred in a tax year; and
- are not used to work out your tax reduction at the basic rate,

can be carried forward to the following year.

## Business loans

Interest on any borrowings by your business can count as a deduction from your business profits for tax purposes. Provided that the borrowed money is issued for business purposes it does not matter whether the interest is paid on:

- a loan taken out for some specific purpose; or
- borrowings because your bank account goes overdrawn.

Interest you pay will also qualify for tax relief where you need to borrow to:

- buy an asset, such as a car or a piece of machinery, for use in your business; or
- purchase a share in a partnership of which you are about to become a member, or contribute capital for use in its business.

Perhaps, however, you have business connections with a private company? Interest paid on a loan raised so you can either buy shares in the company, or lend it money for use in its business, is tax deductible. You must either:

- own at least 5 per cent of the company's share capital; or
- hold at least some shares in the company and spend the greater part of your time working in the business.

Employees who need to borrow to buy shares in their company, as part of an employee buy-out, are allowed tax relief on the interest paid on their borrowings.

## Gift Aid

Gift Aid is an Income Tax relief for cash gifts, without limit, by individuals to charities. Under Gift Aid a charity can claim back from HMRC 25p for every £1 you donate.

With Gift Aid you can give any amount – large or small -– regularly or as a one-off donation. You can also pay via cash, cheque, postal order, standing order, direct debit or by using your credit or debit card.

# Interest payments and other outgoings

For your donation to qualify under Gift Aid you must:

- pay at least as much tax (both Income Tax and CGT) in the tax year in which you make your cash gifts as the charities will reclaim on them; and
- make a declaration to the charity, either orally or in writing, that you want your donation to be regarded as made under Gift Aid.

## Tax Saver

If you pay tax at either the 40 per cent or 45 per cent rates, you can claim tax relief on your Gift Aid donations. This is worked out on the difference between the top rate at which you pay and the basic rate of 20 per cent.

Therefore, for every £100 you donate:

| Your top rate of tax (%) | Your tax saving (£) | What the charity receives (£) |
| --- | --- | --- |
| 40 | 25 | 125 |
| 45 | 31.25 | 131.25 |

---

Norman Walton gave donations totalling £2,400 under Gift Aid in 2024/25. Norman is a higher rate taxpayer so he can reduce his tax bill by £600 as follows:

|  | £ |
| --- | --- |
| Grossed-up donations – £2,400 × (100/80) | 3,000 |
| Tax relief thereon at 40 per cent | 1,200 |
| *Less*: Deducted when making donations | 600 |
| Reduction in Income Tax payable | 600 |

> **Tax Saver**
>
> You can claim to carry back donations so they are treated as if paid in the previous tax year. For example, they can be carried back to 2023/24 so you get the tax relief in that year rather than in 2024/25, provided the donations were:
>
> - made after 5 April 2022; and
> - before 31 January 2025 – or the date when you send your 2023/24 Tax Return to your tax office (if earlier).
>
> The claim must be made in the *first* Tax Return you submit. It will be rejected in any amended return.

## Gifts of assets to charities

> **Tax Saver**
>
> You can claim relief from both Income Tax and Capital Gains Tax at your top rates of both taxes for the full market value of any gifts of shares, securities or land and buildings to charities at the time of the gift.

The assets that qualify for this type of tax relief are:

- shares or securities listed on a recognized Stock Exchange;
- shares or securities dealt in on any market in the United Kingdom that is designated for this purpose by HMRC;
- units in an authorized unit trust;
- shares in an open-ended investment company;
- an interest in an offshore fund; and
- land and buildings.

Jennifer Pickard pays tax at the higher rate of 40 per cent on a substantial part of her income. In September 2024 she decided to give shares in a quoted company valued at £8,000 to her favourite charity. The taxable capital gain on the shares would have been £3,600 if she had sold them. Jennifer saves tax of £3,920 as follows:

|  | £ |
| --- | --- |
| Reduction in Income Tax (40 per cent × £8,000) | 3,200 |
| Capital Gains Tax not payable on the gain* (20 per cent × £3,600) | 720 |
| 2024/25 Maximum tax saving | 3,920 |

*Assuming Jennifer had already used her annual exemption Limit (see Chapter 13).

# Payroll giving

If you are in employment there may be another way that you can make tax-efficient gifts to charity. But, first of all, you need to enquire if your employer participates in such an arrangement through a charity arrangement approved by HMRC. If so you can ask your employer to make regular deductions from your salary that, as part of the scheme, will be passed on to the charities of your choice. You will receive full Income Tax relief on such donations. There is no limit to the amount you can contribute this way each year.

### Tax Saver

To give £100 costs:

- £80 if you pay tax at the basic rate;
- £60 for a higher rate taxpayer; and
- £55 for someone paying tax at the additional rate.

# 05
# Working in employment

Most of us have worked for somebody else at some stage in our lives either on a full-time or part-time basis.

## Am I employed?

Generally speaking you are regarded as employed:

- if you work for the same organization from day to day; and
- you do not have the risks associated with the running of a business.

If the answer is 'yes' to most of the following questions then you will correctly have been categorized as having employee status.

- Do you have to do the work yourself?
- Can you be told where to work, when to work, how to work and what to do?
- Can you be moved from job to job?
- Do you have to work a set number of hours?
- Are you paid a regular wage or salary?
- Can you get additional pay for overtime and a bonus?
- Are you entitled to holiday pay and sickness pay when you are away from work unwell?
- Are you responsible for managing anyone else engaged by your employer?

## Earnings

The earnings from an employment on which Income Tax is payable are:

- a salary or wage;
- a bonus;
- overtime;
- commission;
- tips or gratuities;
- holiday or sick pay;
- part-time earnings;
- director's salary or fees; and
- benefits-in-kind.

## The Pay As You Earn (PAYE) system

The mechanism for collecting the tax due on earnings from an employment is the PAYE system. It is the responsibility of employers to:

- deduct both Income Tax and National Insurance Contributions from the earnings of their employees; and
- pay the total deductions over to HMRC every month.

The PAYE deductions from an employee's earnings are regarded as credit against the total tax payable by the employee for that tax year. Each employee's individual allowances and reliefs are taken into account by the employer in working out the amount of tax to deduct from the employee's salary or wage. This is possible because HMRC issue all employers with a code number for each employee.

## Code numbers

Every employee's annual PAYE Coding Notice sets out:

- on the first lines, the total tax allowances due; and
- on the lines below, the amounts taken away from the allowances.

On the reverse of the form are guidance notes to help you understand how HMRC work out your tax code.

The PAYE system allows for the net allowances to be spread evenly throughout the tax year in working out the deductions for Income Tax so as to avoid any substantial variation to the amount of your regular salary cheque or pay packet.

All things being equal this system should ensure that the right amount of tax is deducted from your earnings each year. However, it can only work properly and effectively if you promptly tell your tax office of changes in your personal circumstances that affect any of the entries on your Notice of Coding. For example, most Coding Notices for the 2024/25 tax year, beginning on 6 April 2024, were sent out during the early part of the year. This is before your tax office will have received your 2023/24 Tax Return, stating your income, capital gains, reliefs and allowances for the year to 5 April 2024. It follows, therefore, that the information on which all 2024/25 code numbers have been based is out of date. This is why it is important that you check your code number for 2024/25 and tell your tax office if:

- alterations are required to your allowances of reliefs;
- you have changed jobs or ceased to be employed;
- you have started receiving a pension;
- there has been a big change in your income; or
- you have moved home.

Once again, tax allowances for 2024/25 are:

|  | £ |
|---|---|
| Personal | 12,570 |
| Transferable marriage | 1,260 |
| Married couples – maximum | 11,080 |
| Married couples – minimum | 4,280 |
| Blind persons | 3,070 |

Figure 5.1 is an illustration of Simon Black's 2024/25 Notice of Coding. Simon is a married man, with two young children.

**Figure 5.1**  Notice of Coding

HM Revenue
& Customs

MR S BLACK
12 CHURCH RISE
BROADWOOD
PT3 8ZL

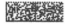   35800

## Dear MR S BLACK

National Insurance number    BZ 62 24 17 A

### This is to tell you your tax code(s) for the year 6 April 2024 to 5 April 2025

Your tax code is used by your employer(s) and/or pension provider(s) to work out how much Income Tax to collect from your pay or pension. We send them a separate tax code notice.

#### This is how we worked out your tax code(s)

| Your tax-free amount | | | For help |
|---|---|---|---|
| Personal Allowance | £12,570 | | Go to note 1 |
| **Total** | £12,570 | | |
| Less Car Benefit | £4,400 | | Go to note 2 |
| Less Car Fuel Benefit | £5,148 | | Go to note 3 |
| Less Medical Insurance | £900 | | Go to note 4 |
| Less Unpaid Tax | £420 | | Go to note 5 |
| **Total tax-free amount** | £1,632 | | |
| Your total tax-free amount is used as follows | | Tax code | For help |
| BROADWOOD ENGINEERS LTD £1,702 of this income is tax-free | | 170 L | Go to note 6 |
| **This totals your tax-free amount**   £1,702 | | | Go to note 7 |

**SOURCE** HMRC

On the first line of the Notice is Simon's personal allowance for 2024/25 of £12,570. The amounts taken away from Simon's allowances are on the lines below. These are as follows.

- The first three deductions are the taxable figures of the benefits-in-kind of a company car, free fuel for private motoring and private medical insurance cover provided to Simon and his family by his employer. The Income Tax payable by Simon on these benefits is, therefore, collected by restricting his allowances by the taxable amount of the benefits.

- The last deduction is for tax of £84 underpaid in 2022/23. For a number of reasons the allowances given, or deductions included, in Simon's Notice of Coding may turn out not to be totally correct. If, as a result, tax is underpaid, this is usually collected in a subsequent year by restricting allowances in the coding. In the illustration a restriction of Simon's 2024/25 allowances by £420 will enable HMRC to collect the underpayment of £84 (£420 @ 20 per cent) from him.

The combined effect of these adjustments is to leave Simon with allowances of just £1,702 to be set against his salary for 2023/24. His code number is 170L. It is not difficult to see that there is a direct link between Simon's allowances and his code number. The suffix letter added to the coding is a way of identifying the category into which a taxpayer falls.

- C indicates you are a taxpayer resident in Wales.
- L is for a code with the basic personal allowance.
- M shows that you have received 10 per cent of your spouse's/partner's personal allowance.
- N tells you that you have transferred 10 per cent of your personal allowance.
- S applies if your main home is in Scotland.*
- OT means that:
  - your personal allowance has been used up;
  - you have started a new job and do not have a form P45; or
  - you fail to provide your new employer with the information needed to give you a tax code.
- T applies in many other cases, for example if:
  - your earnings exceed £100,000 resulting in a reduced personal allowance; or
  - there are items in the coding which need to be reviewed.

* There are five subsidiary tax codes dealing with the amount of tax to be deducted from the earnings of individuals liable to Scottish tax.

There are also a number of other codes.

- BR tells your employer to deduct tax at the basic rate.
- NT means no tax will be deducted.
- D0 means tax will be deducted at the higher rate of 40 per cent.
- D1 means tax will be taken off at the additional rate of 45 per cent.
- K is given to employees whose total deductions including taxable benefits exceed their personal allowances. The amount of the negative allowances is then added to the pay on which tax is payable. The system of K codes ensures that taxpayers pay all the tax due on their excess benefits evenly throughout the tax year under the PAYE system.
- X applies where HMRC will review the tax you have paid after 5 April.

## Emergency tax codes

You may find that you are on an emergency tax code because you have:

- changed jobs;
- moved from self employment to work for someone; or
- started receiving company benefits or the State Pension.

You will know if you are on an emergency tax code if the tax code on your payslip in 2024/25 is:

- 1257L W1;
- 1257L M1;
- 1257L X.

As a result you will pay Income Tax on all your earnings which exceed the 2024/25 personal allowance of £12,570.

An emergency tax code is only temporary. Your employer can help you get on the right tax code.

# How tax is worked out using your tax code

The coding notice issued to Simon Black for 2024/25 tells him that his tax-free amount for the year is £1,702. He earns £43,680 per annum in his job.

The deduction for tax is worked out as follows:

|  | £ |
|---|---|
| Pay from employment | 43,680 |
| *Less*: Tax-free amount for year | 1,702 |
| Tax due on | 41,978 |
| Income Tax payable |  |
| £37,700 @ 20 per cent | 7,540 |
| £4,278 @ 40 per cent | 1,711 |
|  | 9,251 |

To work out the weekly amounts of pay and tax, divide the pay and tax payable for the year by 52:

- Weekly pay is £43,680 ÷ 52 = £840
- Weekly tax is £9,251 ÷ 52 = £177.90

To work out the equivalent monthly amount divide by 12:

- Monthly pay is £43,680 ÷ 12 = £3,640
- Monthly tax is £9,280 ÷ 12 = £770.92

# Form P60

Shortly after the end of each tax year every employer sends HMRC a Return summarizing:

- the names of all employees;
- their earnings during that tax year; and
- the deductions made for both Income Tax and National Insurance Contributions.

**Figure 5.2** Form P60

## P60 End of Year Certificate
**Tax year to 5 April 2024**

### To the employee:
Please keep this certificate in a safe place as you will need it if you have to fill in a tax return. You also need it to make a claim for tax credits and Universal Credit or to renew your claim.

It also helps you check that your employer is using the correct National Insurance number and deducting the right rate of National Insurance contributions.

**By law you are required to tell HM Revenue and Customs about any income that is not fully taxed, even if you are not sent a tax return.**

HM Revenue and Customs

The figures marked should be used for your tax return, if you get one

### Employee's details
| | |
|---|---|
| Surname | FORD |
| Forenames or initials | ANNE |
| National Insurance number | BZ 62 24 17A |
| Works/payroll number | |

### Pay and Income Tax details

| | Pay £ p | Tax deducted £ p |
|---|---|---|
| In previous employments | | |
| In this employment | 37,440 00 | 8,443 00 |
| Total for year | 37,440 00 | 8,443 00 |

If refund mark 'R'

Final tax code: **201 L**

### National Insurance contributions in this employment

| NIC table letter | Earnings at the Lower Earnings Limit (LEL) (where earnings are equal to or exceed the LEL) £ | Earnings above the LEL, up to and including the Primary Threshold (PT) £ | Earnings above the PT, up to and including the Upper Earnings Limit (UEL) £ | Employee's contributions due on all earnings above the PT £ p |
|---|---|---|---|---|
| A | 6,136 | 2,496 | 28,808 | 3,456 96 |
| | | | | |
| | | | | |
| | | | | |

### Statutory payments included in the pay 'In this employment' figure above

| Statutory Maternity Pay £ p | Statutory Paternity Pay £ p | Statutory Shared Parental Pay £ p |
|---|---|---|
| Statutory Adoption Pay £ p | Statutory Parental Bereavement Pay £ p | |

### Other details

**Student Loan deductions** in this employment (whole £s only) £

**Postgraduate Loan deductions** in this employment (whole £s only) £

**To employee**

Your employer's full name and address (including postcode)

Employer PAYE reference

### Certificate by Employer/Paying Office
This form shows your total pay for Income Tax purposes in this employment for the year.

**SOURCE** HMRC

Working in employment

By 31 May following the end of a tax year, your employer must give you your Form P60 on paper or electronically. This is a certificate of your earnings for the past tax year and shows several things.

- How much Income Tax and National Insurance Contributions you paid.
- The Code Number used in working out the deductions for Income Tax.
- Your National Insurance number.
- Your employer's name and address.

Figure 5.2 is an illustration of the Form P60 sent to Anne Ford by her employer for 2024/25. This shows:

- the tax deducted from her earnings of £37,440 in the year amounted to £7,086, based on a tax code of 201L; and
- she made National Insurance Contributions totalling £3,456.96

# Starting work

Your employer will ask you to fill in HMRC's new starter checklist if you:

- are starting a job for the first time;
- have not already been in work during the tax year;
- are also in another job; or
- receive the State Pension or an occupational pension.

The information on the new starter checklist enables your employer to:

- work out your tax code;
- set you up on their payroll software; and
- register you with HMRC.

As a result the right deductions for Income Tax and National Insurance can be made from your wage or salary.

# Moving jobs

Whenever you change your job your old employer will give you Parts 1A, 2 and 3 of Form P45. On this form are:

- your name and address;

- the name and address of your past employer;
- your tax district and reference number;
- your code number at the date of leaving;
- your accumulative salary and the tax deductions for the tax year up to the date that you leave; and
- your salary and tax deductions from the last employment unless this information is the same as the accumulative figures.

Your ex-employer submits the first part of the Form P45 to their tax district online.

Parts 2 and 3 of the Form P45 must be given to your new employer, or Jobcentre Plus if you are not in work.

Your new employer will enter your address and the date you start your new job before sending Part 3 of the form to their own tax office. The information on the form allows your current employer to make the correct deductions for Income Tax and National Insurance from your salary or wage from the date you start your new job.

You should keep Part 1A of the form for your own records because it may be helpful when you come to prepare your own Tax Return.

## Tax-deductible expenses

The rules allowing you to claim tax relief on expenses connected with your employment are extremely restricted. You are denied tax relief on almost all types of expense that are not ultimately borne by your employer. This is because, as an employee, you have to show that any expenditure is incurred 'wholly, exclusively and necessarily' in performing the duties of your employment. If your employer will not foot the bill for the expenditure involved, then HMRC take the view that it was incurred as a matter of choice rather than of necessity. Nevertheless, some business expenses paid personally are deductible from your income and should be claimed on your Tax Return.

### Tax Saver

There are several tax-deductible expenses that can be used.

- Annual subscriptions to a professional body.
- Business use of your own car and telephone.

- Travel and overnight expenses.
- Clothing and upkeep of tools – HMRC and the trade unions have agreed flat-rate allowances for the upkeep of tools and special clothing in most classes of industry. The current rates are set out in Appendix 1. As an alternative you can claim a deduction for the actual amounts spent on these items.
- Payment by directors or employees for work-related insurance cover. Tax relief is also allowed on meeting the cost of uninsured liabilities.

## Tax-free expenses

The cost of most expenses you incur in your work is ultimately met by your employer, who either reimburses you on an expense claim or pays for them direct. There are several tax-free non-financial benefits for employees.

- Free or subsidized meals in a staff canteen, providing the facilities can be used by all staff.
- Sporting and recreational facilities.
- Staff parties, providing the annual cost to the employer is no more than £150 per head.
- Awards for long service of at least 20 years. The cost of the articles purchased by the employer must not exceed £50 for each year of service.
- Gifts not exceeding £250 in the tax year to an employee from a third party by reason of his or her employment.
- One routine health check and one medical screening each year.
- Eye tests and corrective glasses if your employer is required, by law, to provide eye and eyesight tests for you because of the work you do.
- Up to £500 each year for recommended medical treatment, so you can get back to work.
- Work-related training expenses including fees, travel, reasonable subsistence and the cost of any books.
- The cost of out-placement counselling and retraining courses for both full- and part-time employees.
- Payments not exceeding £500 in a tax year by your employer for pensions advice.

- Equipment or facilities provided to disabled people to enable them to carry out their jobs.
- Computer and other office equipment loaned to employees for business use only.
- One mobile telephone per employee for private use.
- Childcare facilities at the workplace or elsewhere (but not on domestic premises).
- Employer-supported childcare of up to £55 a week. For higher and additional rate taxpayers joining an employer's scheme after 5 April 2011 the relief is limited to £28 and £25 respectively. Employers can either contract with an approved child carer or provide childcare vouchers. (No longer available for new entrants.)
- Up to £4 per week paid to you by your employer for working at home as part of your employment contract. You are not required to produce any supporting evidence of the costs you incur.
- Accommodation and subsistence expenses when your duties require you to travel abroad. HMRC have published a list of benchmarks for use by your employer. Only payments in excess of the rates are taxable.
- Personal incidental expenses when you stay away from home overnight on business. The most common expenses covered are newspapers, telephone calls to home and laundry. The tax-free limits, including VAT, are £5 per night for stays anywhere in the United Kingdom and £10 per night elsewhere. Where these limits are exceeded the whole payment becomes payable – not the excess.
- Bicycle and cycling safety equipment made available to employees mainly to get them between home and work.
- Parking facilities for cars, motorbikes or bicycles at or near your place of work.
- A work bus service.
- The cost of a taxi fare when you have been working late and either public transport is no longer available or it would be unreasonable to expect you to use it at a late hour. Infrequent late working means working until at least 9.00 pm not more than 60 times in a tax year.
- The cost of electricity provided in workplace charging points for electric or plug-in hybrid cars and vans owned by employees.
- Mileage allowances where employees use their car, van, motorcycle or pedal cycle on business.

The tax-free rates laid down by HMRC for 2024/25 are:

| Cars and vans | |
|---|---|
| • First 10,000 miles | 45 p per mile |
| • Excess | 25 p per mile |
| Motorcycles | 24 p per mile |
| Bicycles | 20 p per mile |

> **Tax Saver**
>
> Employees are taxed on payments made by their employers over and above the rates in the table, but they can claim back and get tax relief on the difference where their employers pay them less than the permitted rate.

# Employee travel

The cost of travelling between home and work is not allowable for tax purposes, other than for disabled employees who are given financial help by their employers with home-to-work travel on public transport or by some other means.

However, tax relief is allowed on all your business travel where your journey starts from either home or your permanent workplace. Where the full cost of a journey is not reimbursed by your employer, you can claim tax relief on the excess miles not paid for by your employer.

## *(a) Site-based workers*

These are employees who work at a number of different places for periods of a few weeks or months at a time. Travelling expenses reimbursed to them are tax-free providing a few conditions are met.

- The worker initially expects the posting not to exceed two years, and the stay actually does last for less than this time.
- There is no requirement for an employee to return to his or her permanent workplace when each site job comes to an end.
- An employee's work on-site may be considered as a single continuous period even if he or she is occasionally moved off-site.

## (b) Employees with areas

The geographical area covered by employees such as salespeople is treated as their permanent place of work. The following special rules apply.

- All travel within the area is eligible for tax relief.
- Where an employee lives outside his or her area, travel to the start of the area is classified as home-to-work travel and is taxable if paid for by the employer.
- The entire country is likely to be the area for any employee whose duties extend to servicing customers throughout the whole of the United Kingdom.

All travelling appointments of service engineers are treated as business travel qualifying for tax relief.

## (c) More than one workplace

No tax relief is due for travel from home to either place of work for employees with more than one permanent place of location. It is HMRC's view that a workplace is likely to be considered as permanent if:

- an employee regularly performs 40 per cent or more of the duties of their employment there;
- customers, suppliers and others would expect to make contact with the employee there; and
- the employee has an office or desk and support services.

# Home working

The Covid-19 pandemic saw huge numbers of staff working from home. However, the special working from home allowance for Covid-19 has now ceased. You cannot claim tax relief if you choose to work from home. This includes situations where:

- your employment contract lets you work from home some or all of the time;
- you work from home because of Covid-19;
- your employer has an office, but you cannot go there sometimes because it's full.

> **Tax Saver**
>
> However, to get tax benefits, you must be able to demonstrate that you work from home as a necessity rather than by choice. If you satisfy this test you should be able to claim tax relief on:
>
> - a proportion of your household costs such as heating, lighting, telephone and water (if any);
> - use of your car, computer and tools for your employer's business; and
> - other expenses you incur on stationery, books and professional subscriptions for the business.

# Benefits-in-kind

Directors and employees are generally taxed on:

- the actual value of any employment-related benefits; and
- taxable expenses.

However, trivial benefits-in-kind costing no more than £50 each are tax exempt. As well as being less than £50, a trivial benefit-in-kind mustn't be cash or a cash voucher. It also can't be in the terms of an employee's contract, or a reward for work of performance.

There is an annual cap of £300 on these so-called trivial benefits provided to:

- directors or other officer holders of small companies; and
- members of their families and households.

Information about your expense payments and benefits-in-kind is supplied by your employer to your tax office each year on Form P11D. Your employer should give you a copy of this form by 6 July following the end of the tax year. It sets out your employer's calculations of your taxable payments and cash equivalents of benefits-in-kind. It is up to you to claim those that are not taxable. This should not cause you any problem where expenses such as travelling and entertaining have genuinely arisen from the performance of the duties of your employment.

There are set rules for calculating some benefits.

## (a) Company cars

For many employees the company car continues to be an important part of the remuneration package. The system of taxing company cars is geared towards encouraging the cleaner use of cars by linking the tax charge to the exhaust emission of the car.

When the time comes for you to change your company car it will pay you to look into the carbon dioxide ($CO_2$) emission of the proposed replacement. As you will see from the following table you will save tax on your company car benefit by opting for a car with a lower approved $CO_2$ emission figure.

The tax charge is based on a percentage of the list price of a car (including qualifying accessories) but graduated according to the level of the car's carbon dioxide emissions. The minimum charge is 13 per cent of list price, increasing to a maximum of 37 per cent if $CO_2$ emissions are above the prescribed level.

In view of their higher emissions of pollutants, diesel cars are subject to a 4 per cent supplementary charge. However, even for diesel cars the maximum charge cannot exceed 37 per cent of a car's price. Include the following:

If you drive a car with very low emissions, such as a hybrid or electric car, then this will also be factored in. For company cars with emissions of 1 to 50g/km, the value of the car is based on its zero emissions mileage or 'electric range'. This is the distance the car can drive before needing to recharge. Contact your employer to determine this value.

Following a change in how it calculates emissions-related taxes in April 2020, the UK government is currently using two tax tables, depending on when your car was made. Vehicles registered prior to 6 April 2020 have one set of rates and vehicles built after 6 April 2020 have a different set.

However, this is set to change. In the Autumn Budget 2024 it was announced that the appropriate percentage used to calculate company car tax, in respect of emissions, is set to change.

From 2028 to 2029, and 2029 to 2030, this will rise by 2 per cent a year.

Vehicles with $CO_2$ emissions of 1g to 50g per kilometre will have appropriate percentages of 18 per cent in 2028 to 2029 and 19 per cent in 2029 to 2030.

The appropriate percentages for all other emission bands will increase by 1 percentage point per year in 2028 to 2029 and 2029 to 2030. This will be to a maximum appropriate percentage of 38 per cent for 2028 to 2029 and 39 per cent for 2029 to 2030.

**Working in employment** 51

The car benefit charges for cars with an approved $CO_2$ emissions figure are as follows:

Company Car Tax BIK rates (models registered after 6 April 2021)

| $CO_2$ emissions (g/km) | Electric range (miles) | BIK rate 2023/24 % | BIK rate 2024/25 % | BIK rate 2025/26 % |
|---|---|---|---|---|
| 0 | N/A | 2 | 2 | 3 |
| 1–50 | >130 | 2 | 2 | 3 |
| 1–50 | 70–129 | 5 | 5 | 6 |
| 1–50 | 40–69 | 8 | 8 | 9 |
| 1–50 | 30–39 | 12 | 12 | 13 |
| 1–50 | <30 | 14 | 14 | 15 |
| 51–54 | | 15 | 15 | 16 |
| 55–59 | | 16 | 16 | 17 |
| 60–64 | | 17 | 17 | 18 |
| 65–69 | | 18 | 18 | 19 |
| 70–74 | | 19 | 19 | 20 |
| 75–79 | | 20 | 20 | 21 |
| 80–84 | | 21 | 21 | 22 |
| 85–89 | | 22 | 22 | 23 |
| 90–94 | | 23 | 23 | 24 |
| 95–99 | | 24 | 24 | 25 |
| 100–104 | | 25 | 25 | 26 |
| 105–109 | | 26 | 26 | 27 |
| 110–114 | | 27 | 27 | 28 |
| 115–119 | | 28 | 28 | 29 |
| 120–124 | | 29 | 29 | 30 |
| 125–129 | | 30 | 30 | 31 |
| 130–134 | | 31 | 31 | 32 |
| 135–139 | | 32 | 32 | 33 |
| 140–144 | | 33 | 33 | 34 |
| 145–149 | | 34 | 34 | 35 |
| 150–154 | | 35 | 35 | 36 |

| $CO_2$ emissions (g/km) | Electric range (miles) | BIK rate 2023/24 % | BIK rate 2024/25 % | BIK rate 2025/26 % |
|---|---|---|---|---|
| 155–159 | | 36 | 36 | 37 |
| 160–164 | | 37 | 37 | 37 |
| 165–169 | | 37 | 37 | 37 |
| 170+ | | 37 | 37 | 37 |

> **Tax Saver**
>
> Sometimes it is better to own your own car and charge your employer for the cost of all your business mileage. But you must keep a proper and detailed log of all business and private mileage.

Mileage between home and work counts as private, not business, usage except in a car made available to an employee who:

- has a travelling appointment;
- travels from home to a temporary place of work if the distance travelled is less than the distance between the normal place of work and the temporary place of work; or
- is a home worker and travels from home to another place of work in the performance of his or her duties.

There are several other circumstances where home-to-work travel in an employer-provided car is considered to be private use but is disregarded for tax purposes. These are where the car is provided:

- to a disabled person for home-to-work travel and there is no other private use;
- for home-to-work travel when public transport is disrupted; and
- for late-night journeys home from work.

This will not have an impact on 2024/25 but it's worth highlighting that in the 2024 Autumn Budget the chancellor announced that rates for how company cars are taxed will be changed from 2028/29 and 2029/30.

## (b) Fuel benefits

If your employer pays for fuel for your private motoring, this also gives rise to a taxable benefit on which you have to pay Income Tax. The taxable amount is calculated on the car benefit percentage for the $CO_2$ emissions of your car multiplied by 27,800. So if the car benefit percentage for your car is 23 per cent, the taxable benefit is 23 per cent of 27,800 which is £6,394.

The benefit is:

- reduced to zero if the full cost of fuel for all your private motoring is reimbursed to your employer;
- proportionately reduced if you stop enjoying the use of free fuel for non-business motoring part way through a tax year; and
- not charged for any period of at least 30 days during which your car cannot be used or is unavailable to you.

> **Tax Saver**
>
> You will often be better off paying for your own fuel for non-business mileage.

## (c) Company vans

If your employer provides you with a company van in 2024/25 without any unrestricted use, no matter the age or size of the van:

- you are taxed on a fixed amount of £3,960;
- for a company van with zero emission the benefit is 80 per cent of the fixed charge – this is equivalent to a taxable amount of £3,168;
- there is an additional benefit of £757 where your employer pays for fuel for private mileage.

## (d) Pooled vehicles

The private use of a car from an employer's pool of vehicles will not give rise to a tax charge on an employee provided:

- any home-to-work travel is merely incidental to business use; and
- the vehicle is not garaged at or near the employee's home overnight.

## (e) Living accommodation

In some trades it is established practice for an employer to provide living accommodation. This can also be desirable where there is a security risk. No Income Tax liability arises in either set of circumstances.

In other situations Income Tax is chargeable on the annual value of the property after deducting any rent paid for it. For these purposes the annual valuation is broadly equivalent to the gross rateable value. Estimated rateable values will be used for new properties not appearing on the domestic rating list.

An additional tax charge arises where the accommodation costs more than £75,000. This is worked out by applying HMRC's official interest rate (see below) to the excess of the cost price above £75,000.

## (f) Beneficial loans

The rules dealing with interest-free or low-rate-interest loans from an employer are as follows.

- The taxable benefit is worked out by applying HMRC's official rate of interest to the loan, currently 2.25 per cent.
- Any interest actually paid on the loan reduces the amount of the benefit.
- No tax charge arises where all of an employee's cheap or interest-free loans, excluding loans that qualify for tax relief, total less than £10,000.
- There is no tax charge where the loan is for a purpose on which the interest would qualify for tax relief (see Chapter 4).

## (g) Medical insurance

You will be taxed on the cost of private medical insurance premiums paid by your employer for you or other members of your family. Not subject to tax is the cost of medical insurance cover, or actual medical treatment overseas, while away on business.

## (h) Relocation expenses

An employee who changes job, or is relocated by his or her employer, is not taxed on the costs of a relocation package up to £8,000. This limit applies to each job-related move. There are specific definitions for the removal expenses and benefits that qualify for exemption within the monetary limit.

# Employee share ownership

There are a variety of share, profit sharing and share option schemes, all offering different investment limits and tax reliefs – some more generous than others. Membership of whatever scheme is operated by your employer may be an attractive long-term investment with built-in tax advantages.

## (a) Under a Share Incentive Plan

- Under a Share Incentive Plan, employers can give employees up to £3,600 of shares free of Income Tax and National Insurance. There are several important considerations to be aware of, however.
- Some or all of these shares can be awarded to employees for reaching performance targets.
- Employees are able to buy partnership shares out of their pre-tax salary or wage up to a maximum of 10 per cent of salary or £1,800 a year, whichever is lower, free of Income Tax and National Insurance.
- Employers can match partnership shares by giving employees up to two free shares for each partnership share they buy.
- Employees who sell their shares are liable to Capital Gains Tax only on any increase in the value of their shares after they come out of a plan.
- Free and matching shares must normally be kept in the plan for at least three years – employees can take partnership shares out of the plan at any time.
- Shares must come out of the plan when employees leave and some employees may lose their free and matching shares if they leave their jobs within three years of getting the shares.
- Dividends, up to £1,500 annually, paid on the shares are tax-free providing they are reinvested in additional shares in the company and retained for at least three years.
- Employees who keep their shares in a plan for five years pay no Income Tax or National Insurance on those shares.
- Employees who take their shares out of a plan after three years pay Income Tax and National Insurance on no more than the initial value of the shares – any increase in the value of their shares while in the plan is free of Income Tax and National Insurance.

- Capital Gains Tax roll-over relief is available for existing shareholders of smaller companies who want to sell their shares to a new plan trust to be used for the benefit of employees.

## (b) The main features of a Savings-Related Share Option Scheme

- A Savings-Related Share Option Scheme operates in combination with either a bank or building society 'save as you earn' savings contract. Under this, employees save a fixed regular amount each month and the following applies.
- The maximum amount that can be saved is £500 per month over either a three- or five-year period.
- The price at which options can be offered to directors and employees cannot be less than 80 per cent of the market value of the shares at the time the options are granted.
- The receipt of the options and any increase in the value of the shares between the time that the options are granted and the date when they are exercised are free of Income Tax.

## (c) Under an Approved Profit-Sharing Scheme

- With an Approved Profit-Sharing Scheme, a company makes an allocation of profits to trustees. In turn, these trustees use the contribution in acquiring shares in the company that are subsequently allotted to employees. There are two important considerations to be mindful of.
- The limit on the market value of shares that may be appropriated to any one individual in each tax year is 10 per cent of salary (or £1,800 each year, which is less to buy shares), with a minimum limit of £3,000 and a maximum of £8,000.
- There is no Income Tax liability when the shares are set aside or if they are retained by the trustees of the scheme for three years.

## (d) Inland Revenue Approved Share Option Plan

- With an Inland Revenue Approved Share Option Plan, no liability to Income Tax is imposed on a director or employee who acquires or disposes of ordinary share under such a plan. The following are the key points to remember.
- The market value of shares, at the time of the grant of the option, over which an individual holds unexercised rights under the plan must not

exceed £60,000 (or £30,000 if the options were granted before 6 April 2023).
- An option must be exercised not less than three, or more than 10, years after it is granted, or under three years after a previous exercise.
- The gain is measured by the difference between the sale proceeds and the cost of acquiring the shares, and is charged to Capital Gains Tax at the time of disposal.
- The price payable must be fixed at the time of the grant and must not be less than the market value of the shares at that date.

## (e) *Employee shareholder shares*

- Employee shareholders are either issued or allotted shares worth a minimum of £2,000 in consideration of an employee shareholder agreement. The following key points apply.
- You will not get tax relief if you, or someone you're connected with like a spouse or family member, have 25 per cent or more voting rights in the company.
- For Income Tax purposes employee shareholders will be deemed to have paid £2,000 for their shares, thereby reducing the tax charge at the time of issue or allotment.
- You only pay Capital Gains Tax on gains in excess of £100,000 that you realize during your lifetime.

# Enterprise Management Incentives

Enterprise Management Incentives are aimed at:

- helping small companies attract and retain the key people they need; and
- rewarding employees for taking a risk by investing their time and skills in helping small companies achieve their potential.

Normally, without any charge to Income Tax or National Insurance, companies can grant share options to employees worth up to £250,000 over a three-year period.

A qualifying employee is one who must spend at least 25 hours a week, or if less, 75 per cent of his or her working time on the business of that company.

# Payments on termination of employment

It is often the practice for an employee to be paid a lump sum on the termination of an employment, which can comprise any of the following:

- outstanding salary or wages;
- holiday pay;
- redundancy pay;
- a payment in lieu of notice; and
- compensation for loss of office.

Such payments, which are free of tax, are where:

- the employment ceases because of the accidental death, injury or disability of the employee; or
- most of the employee's time was spent working overseas for the employer.

Otherwise it is necessary to split the award between income from the employment and the remainder.

The amount to be treated as earnings is the 'post-employment notice pay', the calculation of which is not entirely straightforward.

Of the remainder the first £30,000 (including any statutory or contractual redundancy pay) is tax-free, and the excess over this is taxable.

It is not unusual for redundancy and employment termination settlements to provide for benefits, such as membership of a company medical insurance scheme, to continue after the employment has come to an end. Such payments and benefits are taxed only to the extent that they actually arise, and in the year in which they are received or enjoyed.

> Belinda Morrison was made redundant in May 2023. Under her employment termination settlement she received non-employment notice pay lump sum payments of £26,000 and £20,000 on 23 May 2023 and 9 April 2024 respectively. She was also permitted to retain her membership of her employer's company medical insurance scheme for four years at an annual cost to her employer of £1,000. Belinda's total redundancy package for 2023/24 comes to £27,000. As this is below the £30,000 exemption limit she does not pay tax on any part of the package she received in 2023/24. The balance of the exemption limit of £3,000 is carried forward to 2024/25 to be set against the cash payment of £20,000 and the medical insurance benefit of £1,000. For 2024/25, therefore, Belinda's old employer will deduct tax on £18,000.

# 06
# Value Added Tax

Value Added Tax (VAT) is a system for taxing what people spend. It is also administered by HMRC. The National Advice Service (NAS) is the main contact point for businesses. The NAS telephone number is 0300 200 3700.

## What is VAT?

VAT is a self-assessed tax charged on:

- the supply of goods and services in the United Kingdom; and
- the import of goods and certain services into the United Kingdom.

It applies where a taxable person in business makes supplies that are taxable supplies.

## Rates of VAT

There are three rates of VAT: a standard rate of 20 per cent, a reduced rate of 5 per cent and a zero rate. Most of the goods and services supplied in the United Kingdom are liable to tax at the standard rate. Among the goods and services liable at the two lower rates supplies charged at 5 per cent and zero-rated supplies.

Supplies charged at 5 per cent include:

- domestic fuel and power;
- renovations and alterations of eligible dwellings;
- some residential conversions;
- car and booster seats for children; and
- motorcycle and cycle helmets.

Zero-rated supplies include:

- food sold in shops;
- books, magazines and newspapers;
- babywear;
- children's clothing and footwear;
- construction of new homes;
- passenger transport; and
- motorbike and pedal cycle helmets.

## Exempt supplies

Some goods and services have no VAT on them. These include:

- education and training;
- health and welfare;
- insurance;
- land; and
- finance services and banking.

If you sell goods or supply services that are exempt:

- you do not charge VAT on your income; and
- you cannot recover VAT incurred on the purchases and expenses of your business.

Special rules apply where your business makes both chargeable and exempt supplies.

However, from 1 January 2025 there is a change coming to the education exemption under VAT.

As announced in the Autumn Budget 2024, after this date all education services and vocational training provided by private schools in the UK for a charge will be subject to VAT at the standard rate of 20 per cent.

## Registration

If you are just starting up a business it is unlikely you will need to register for VAT immediately. Only when the value of your taxable supplies reaches £90,000 (this was increased from £85,000 on 1 April 2024) in a 'rolling'

# Value Added Tax

12-month period is it compulsory to apply for registration. In working out the turnover of your business for this purpose, remember that taxable supplies are not just those liable at the standard rate but include supplies liable to tax at the lower rates of 5 per cent and zero.

You also need to register if the taxable supplies of your business in the next 30 days are likely to exceed the registration limit of £90,000. Also, do not delay making an application for registration if you acquire an existing business where the previous owner was VAT registered. Sometimes it is possible for you to take on the same registration number as that of the previous owner.

> Simon Potter started up in business in August 2020. He has been successful in building up his turnover each month. Looking back from the end of January 2024, his turnover for the previous 12 months was £80,000. But when he did the same exercise a month later this figure had increased to £95,000. Simon had to notify liability to register by 31 March 2024 and was registered for VAT from 1 April 2024.

You can apply for VAT registration by either using HMRC's online services or downloading Form VAT1 and sending the completed form in by post.

Applying online:

- is easier, faster and more secure;
- is certain as you get an immediate acknowledgement that your application has been received by HMRC; and
- allows you to access your certificate of registration through the 'Your HMRC services' page.

When you register you will be sent a VAT registration certificate confirming:

- your VAT number;
- when you need to submit your VAT Return; and
- the date of your first payment.

It also shows your effective date of registration, which is:

- the date you went over the threshold; or
- the date from which you requested voluntary registration (see below).

Until you get your VAT number you must not charge, or show, VAT on your invoices. But you will still need to pay over the VAT to HMRC for this period.

> **Tax Saver**
>
> It is a good idea to put up your prices to allow for this. Just tell your customers the reason for the increase. When you know your VAT number you can then reissue the invoices detailing the VAT.

You can avoid registration:

- if your taxable turnover temporarily goes above the threshold for registration; and
- you can show evidence why you believe it will not exceed the de-registration threshold of £88,000 in the next year.

# Voluntary registration

Sometimes there are benefits from VAT registration even though the turnover of your business is below the compulsory limit for registration. Voluntary registration is allowed providing you can show that you are, or will be, making some taxable supplies.

> **Tax Saver**
>
> An advantage of voluntary registration is that you can reduce your costs by recovering VAT incurred on your business expenses, including VAT paid on certain start-up costs such as computers and printers.

Voluntary registration is also beneficial where:

- customers will only deal with a supplier who is registered for VAT; or
- the image of your business will be enhanced.

But if your customers are the general public, voluntary registration is unlikely to be to your advantage. They cannot recover the VAT charged on your goods and services so you may be putting yourself at a price disadvantage compared to your competitors.

# Cancellation of registration

You can apply to HMRC to de-register your business from VAT where the taxable turnover falls below the de-registration threshold of £88,000.

De-registration is compulsory where you cease to trade or sell your business.

# Help from HMRC

Telephone support is available on the VAT, Customs and Excise Helpline at 0300 200 3700. You can also get help with VAT by using videos, webinars, online courses and email updates from HMRC.

You should also find the VAT notices and leaflets published by HMRC useful in helping you understand and deal with VAT aspects of your business. Some of these, available from the NAS, are listed in Appendix 2.

# VAT invoices

There is a lot of mandatory information you must show on all VAT invoices issued by your business, whether paper or electronic. This includes:

- the date of issue;
- a sequential number that uniquely identifies the invoice;
- your VAT identification number;
- the full name and address of both your own business and that of your customer;
- a description of the quantity and nature of the goods supplied or services rendered;
- the time of the supply;
- the net unit price;
- the gross amount payable, excluding VAT;
- the rate of VAT charged; and
- the amount of VAT payable.

There are also other specific requirements but these only apply in certain circumstances such as supplies to and from EU countries.

Alternatively you can agree with your customers that they will raise the invoices for the goods or services you have supplied to them. This practice is known as self-billing.

Simplified and modified invoices can be issued for supplies of retail goods under, and over, £250 respectively.

# Records, accounting and Returns

If your business is VAT registered you must do several things.

- Render tax invoices for all taxable supplies of goods and services.
- Retain copies of all VAT invoices issued and received, filed in an orderly manner.
- Maintain proper business and accounting records and keep them for at least six years.
- Maintain an account showing the calculations of your VAT liability for each VAT period.
- Make timely VAT Returns and payments to HMRC.

The VAT payable, or repayable, each period is the simple difference between your VAT output tax and input tax. Output tax is what you charge on the goods and services (outputs) to your customers. Input tax is what you incur on the purchases and expenses (inputs) of running your business.

Totalling the VAT on your outputs and inputs each month should make it fairly straightforward to bring together the information you need to complete the VAT Return – Form VAT100 – for the accounting periods shown on your registration certificate.

---

Beth Way runs a hairdressing salon which is VAT registered. She has been given quarterly VAT accounting periods in line with the calendar quarters. She accounts for VAT as a retailer on the basis of the income received each quarter. Her VAT account for the three months to the end of March 2024 was:

|  | £ | £ |
| --- | --- | --- |
| **Output Tax** | | |
| January | 1,940 | |
| February | 1,830 | |
| March | 2,070 | |
| Total | 5,840 | 5,840 |
| **Input Tax** | | |
| January | 220 | |
| February | 160 | |
| March | 250 | |
| Total | 630 | 630 |
| **Net amount due to HMRC** | | 5,210 |

The various boxes on your VAT Return can be filled in from the figures in your VAT account and the tax-exclusive values of your outputs and inputs for the period.

Make sure you submit each Return and pay what is due to HMRC within the stipulated time limit. If the VAT you have reclaimed on the purchases and expenses of the business exceeds the VAT on your turnover for the period, the Return will show you are entitled to a repayment, which will be sent direct to your bank account within 30 days of HMRC receiving your VAT Return.

If you wish, you can request that your quarterly VAT Return periods coincide with your financial year.

# Online filing of Returns

All businesses, irrespective of their turnover, must:

- file VAT Returns online; and
- pay any VAT due electronically.

There are a number of benefits from online filing such as up to an extra seven days to:

- file your Return; and
- pay any VAT due.

To pay by Direct Debit, the internet, telephone or BACS Direct Payment you need the following information:

Sort code: 08-32-00

Account number: 11963155

Account name: HMRC VAT

Quote your VAT registration number leaving no gaps.

You can always look at your VAT online account to find out if your payment is on your record. It should be updated within 48 hours of receipt.

When signing up for online filing you should have provided an email address and set up an email reminder. This will be the only communication to you from HMRC that it is now time to complete a Return.

## Making VAT Digital

Making Tax Digital for VAT means that if your business has a taxable income above the requirement for VAT registration it must keep records in digital form and file the VAT Returns using software.

As a result the software which your business uses must be able to:

- keep and maintain the records set out in the covering regulations;
- prepare your VAT Returns using the information kept in these digital records; and
- communicate with HMRC digitally via the specific Interface platform.

These rules apply for your first VAT period starting on or after 1 April 2019.

## Input tax

The actual amount of input tax on purchases does not matter quite so much when the Flat Rate Scheme is used (see page 69). For other businesses it is only the input tax on the costs of the business that can be claimed when VAT Returns are completed. Sometimes expenses may be incurred where input tax cannot be claimed at all. Examples include business entertaining and private purchases paid for through your business.

Occasionally there may be a need to apportion input tax, such as that on home telephone bills incurred partly for business and partly for private purposes. Apportionment is best done on a percentage basis which, provided it is reasonable, HMRC can be expected to accept.

> **Tax Saver**
>
> You can also recover VAT paid on certain purchases made by your business before it was registered for VAT. But there is a time limit for back-dating claims, which is:
>
> - four years for goods you still own, or which were used in making other goods you still have; and
> - six months for services.
>
> The goods and services:
>
> - must relate to the purpose of the business; and
> - you can reclaim the VAT on them on your first VAT Return.

## Motor cars and fuel

Businesses directly concerned with motoring, such as new car dealers, vehicle hirers, taxi drivers or driving schools, may be able to reclaim all input tax on cars that they buy or lease. Input tax cannot be claimed back on cars bought by other businesses and made available for private use. However, it may be possible to claim 50 per cent of the input tax on the rental payments where cars are leased.

There are two alternative methods for dealing with input tax on motor fuel.

- The first is all input tax is claimed and a fixed scale charge to take account of private use is applied. From 1 May 2024 the fuel scale charges, based on a 20 per cent rate, for a three-month period are as shown in the table.
- The second is no input tax is claimed and the fixed-scale charge is ignored. If you intend to deal with motor fuel this way you should write to HMRC to tell them.

Input tax on repairs and maintenance of business cars can be claimed whichever way you decide to deal with motor fuel.

Quarterly scale charges for 2024/25

| CO$_2$ emissions in g/km | Quarterly scale charge (£) |
| --- | --- |
| 120 or below | 174 |
| 125 | 263 |
| 130 | 279 |
| 135 | 297 |
| 140 | 315 |
| 145 | 332 |
| 150 | 350 |
| 155 | 368 |
| 160 | 385 |
| 165 | 403 |
| 170 | 420 |
| 175 | 437 |
| 180 | 455 |
| 185 | 473 |
| 190 | 490 |
| 195 | 508 |
| 200 | 526 |
| 205 | 544 |
| 210 | 560 |
| 215 | 578 |
| 220 | 596 |
| 225 and above | 613 |

# Bad debts

Late or non-payment of bills can often have a serious impact on both the cashflow and profitability of a business. When it comes to bad debts it is only when a debt is more than six months old (from the date the payment was due) that an adjustment can be made to recover VAT accounted for on that debt in a previous VAT Return. The debt must be less than four years and six months old.

Adjustments for bad debts, although not separately shown on VAT Returns, must be recorded separately in the VAT account of your business. Listings must be maintained to support both the entries and any further adjustments made to reflect subsequent amounts recovered.

All this information must be retained for four years.

## Special schemes for retailers

Retailers often sell a mixture of both positive and zero-rated goods but do not know how much of each of them is sold from day to day. When this happens they can use one of the schemes available to help them work out their VAT liabilities. If you are in retailing, you should study the leaflets telling you about the various schemes so that you do not pay too much tax.

Where retailers only sell goods that are liable at the standard rate of 20 per cent, the amount of tax included in the gross takings for a period is 1/6. Referred to as the 'VAT fraction', this calculation is worked out as follows:

|  | £ |
|---|---|
| Tax-exclusive value (say) | 100 |
| *Add:* VAT @ 20 per cent | 20 |
| Tax-inclusive price | 120 |
| The VAT included in the tax-inclusive price is therefore | $\left(\dfrac{20}{120}\right) = \left(\dfrac{1}{6}\right)$ |

For goods liable at the reduced rate of 5 per cent the 'VAT fraction' is 1/21.

## Flat Rate Scheme

### Tax Saver

The scheme is open to small businesses whose annual taxable turnover (not including VAT) does not exceed £150,000. It will be of particular appeal to businesses that do not want to spend too much time and effort dealing with all the administrative complications of normal VAT accounting.

Under the scheme, VAT is still charged to customers at the rate appropriate to the supplies made by the business. When you come to complete your VAT Returns there are three important points to keep in mind.

- You do not make a separate claim to recover input tax on purchases, expenses or low-value assets acquired for your business.
- Input tax on a single purchase of a capital asset with a value of more than £2,000, including VAT, can be separately recovered.
- You work out the tax due by applying a fixed percentage to the VAT inclusive turnover of your business for the period.

The percentages have been set by HMRC according to the principal activity of a business and take into account that input tax on normal purchases is not claimed.

> Yvonne Spencer is a hairdresser. Her VAT inclusive turnover for the quarter to the end of March 2024 was £18,000. The VAT flat rate for hairdressers and beauty services is 13 per cent. Yvonne must pay VAT of £2,340 as follows:
>
> £18,000 × 13 per cent = £2,340

Businesses are being strongly encouraged by HMRC to use the scheme, so much so that a 1 per cent reduction in the percentages for the first year is available to new businesses:

- that register for VAT when they should; and
- apply to use the scheme at the same time.

You have to leave the scheme if on the anniversary of your joining, your turnover in the last 12 months was more than £230,000 including VAT or you expect it to be in the next 12 months. Similarly, you have to leave if you expect your total income in the next 30 days alone to be more than £230,000 including VAT.

# Cash accounting

Under the cash accounting scheme:

- you account for VAT on your outputs when you are paid for sales made by your business, rather than by reference to the date of your tax invoices; and

- you reclaim the VAT on your purchases and business expenses when you pay for them.

Your business is eligible to use this scheme from the beginning of a VAT tax period if:

- you expect the value of your taxable supplies (excluding VAT) during the forthcoming year to be no more than £1.35 million; and
- you are not in arrears in submitting past VAT Returns at the time you decide to join the scheme.

You must come out of cash accounting if:

- the amount of your taxable supplies exceeds £1.6 million (exclusive of VAT) in a period of one year; or
- your business fails to comply with the correct requirements for record keeping.

## Annual accounting

Under the annual accounting scheme your business:

- submits just one VAT Return each year;
- makes interim payments of VAT based on an estimate of your liability for the year; and
- completes and sends in its VAT Return two months after the end of the year.

At the same time you can pay over the balance of VAT due and can use it together with both the cash accounting and flat rate schemes.

You can apply online to use the scheme if you reasonably believe that the amount of your taxable supplies, excluding VAT, in the period of 12 months from the date of your application will not exceed £1.35 million. If you are accepted onto the scheme, the start date for the new arrangements will be the first day of your current accounting period. You will be notified in writing if your application has been accepted. The letter you receive will also tell you the amount and timing of your interim payments, and the due date of the Annual Return and balancing payment.

> Vince Charles is in business as a vehicle repairer and is registered for VAT. In October 2024 he applies to use the annual accounting scheme. His quarterly period runs from 1 September to 30 November. His first annual accounting period starts on 1 September 2024 and ends on 31 August 2025.

Once you are in the scheme you can remain in it until your annual turnover exceeds £1.6 million. You will then be taken off the scheme at the end of your current accounting year. Alternatively, if you want to come out of the scheme and go back to the normal method of paying and accounting for VAT you just need to tell HMRC of your decision.

## VAT visits and inspections

VAT officers can visit your business to look at your VAT records. They can also make sure that you are paying or reclaiming the correct amount of VAT.

HMRC usually contact you to arrange a visit and let you know:

- what information they want to look at;
- how long the visit should take; and
- whether they need to inspect your premises.

They normally give you seven days' notice. Afterwards you will get a letter from HMRC about:

- what, if anything, you must do to improve your records for VAT;
- any amendments you must make to your VAT account;
- under or over payments of VAT; and
- any penalty you need to pay.

## Penalties, surcharges and interest

The penalty regime covering VAT aspects of your business extends to:

- failing to register for VAT on time; and
- errors in documents or Returns.

Penalties for errors in documents are calculated:

- as a percentage of the additional tax due; and
- when the inaccuracy is put right.

The penalty is a percentage of the extra tax due and depends on the reason for the inaccuracy as follows:

## Value Added Tax

|  | Rate of penalty | |
| --- | --- | --- |
| **Reason** | **Maximum** | **Minimum** |
| Reasonable care | 30% | No Penalty |
| Deliberate | 70% | 20% |
| Deliberate and concealed | 100% | 30% |

As you can see there is a substantial difference between the minimum and maximum rates of penalty. Therefore, even if you have adjusted for any error on the next VAT Return after it was identified, you should also:

- disclose the error with full details by writing to HMRC before it is picked up by them;
- help HMRC calculate the extra VAT due; and
- allow HMRC to look at any records requested to check on the accuracy of the figures.

By doing all of this you should be able to secure a much reduced level of penalty.

Where a disclosure is made following a prompt from HMRC, the minimum levels of penalty are increased as follows:

|  | **Rate** |
| --- | --- |
| Carelessness | 10%/20%* |
| Deliberate | 35% |
| Deliberate and concealed | 50% |

*Depending on whether the non-deliberate event took place within or after 12 months of the tax being due.

Furthermore, default interest will normally be charged when assessments for errors are issued.

Late submission penalties work on a points-based system. You receive a penalty point for each return you submit late. Once you've reached a penalty point threshold, you'll receive a £200 penalty. You'll then be charged a further £200 penalty for each subsequent late submission while you're at the threshold.

The penalty point threshold is set by your accounting period. The threshold is the maximum points you can receive.

If your accounting period is annual, your penalty points threshold is 2, if your accounting period is quarterly, your threshold is 4 and if your accounting period is monthly, your threshold is 5.

> Here is an example of how it works: Company ABC submits its VAT return quarterly. This means the penalty points threshold is 4.
>
> ABC already has 3 penalty points because it submitted three previous returns late. It submits the next return late and gets a fourth penalty point. The company has now reached its penalty point threshold and has to pay a £200 penalty.

## Penalties if you pay late

The VAT default surcharge has been replaced by new penalties for late payment of VAT.

Late payment interest is charged from the first day that the payment is overdue until the day it's paid in full. The interest rate is Bank of England base rate plus 2.5 per cent.

If payment is more than 15 days late, you'll also be asked to pay a late payment penalty. This starts at 2 per cent of the VAT you owe at day 15. Here is a table:

| Length of overdue period | First late payment penalty | Second late payment penalty |
| --- | --- | --- |
| Payment is up to 15 days overdue | None | None |
| Payment between 16 and 30 days overdue | 2 per cent on the VAT you owe at day 15 | None |
| Payment 31 days or more overdue | 2 per cent of what was outstanding at day 15 Plus 2 per cent of what is still outstanding at day 30 | A daily rate of 4 per cent per year on the outstanding balance Charged every day from 31 until the outstanding balance is paid in full |

# Appeals

You have the right to appeal to an independent tribunal against:

- the imposition of a penalty;
- the amount of a penalty; and
- a decision not to suspend a penalty.

Alternatively you can opt for an internal review by an independent HMRC officer. This is a quick and inexpensive way to resolve any dispute.

# Complaints

VAT officers are committed to the same standards as Tax staff (see the Service Commitment reproduced in Chapter 1), and are expected to abide by them. If you ever feel dissatisfied with the manner in which the affairs of your business have been handled, or think that an officer has overstepped the mark and has exceeded his or her authority, you can write to:

- the person who is in overall charge at the HMRC office for your business; or
- the Complaints Unit for the area where your business is situated.

If you are unable to resolve your complaint satisfactorily your next step is to contact the Adjudicator's Office, which is the independent body set up specifically for this purpose.

# 07
# Working for yourself

If you run your own business, other than through a company or in partnership, you are classified as self-employed for tax purposes. Your business might be a trade, profession or vocation.

## Am I self-employed?

The main distinguishing factor between having self-employed status and working as an employee is the existence of a 'master–servant' relationship. Sometimes it is difficult to draw a line between:

- employment (a contract for service); and
- self-employment (a contract for services).

Your business will be self-employment if the following apply.

- You are responsible for the success or failure of your business.
- You are paid a fixed fee or price for your work.
- You have several customers at the same time.
- You can hire other people at your own expense to help you or to do the work for you.
- You can decide how, when and where the work should be undertaken.
- You can dictate the hours you work.
- You provide your own tools.
- You have no entitlement to paid holidays or sick leave.

You do not have to formalize any business relationship by entering into a contract for the supply of goods or services. Nevertheless, having a contract makes sound business sense because it will cover matters other than those just relative to the taxation consequences of the relationship.

## Starting up in business

Your business is now up and running. It is important that you quickly learn what to do about Tax, National Insurance (see Chapter 8) and maybe Value Added Tax (see Chapter 6).

I suggest you use the online tax registration service to tell HMRC about your new business. You will find this at http://www.gov.uk/new-business-register-for-tax. As part of the registration process you will be asked if you would like to receive business advisory emails. HMRC recognizes that starting and running a business is challenging. By signing up for this free service you will receive a series of tax-related help and support emails.

Other useful services offered by HMRC include:

- free online webinar presentations allowing you to attend seminars without leaving your desk;
- e-learning which you can use whenever it suits you, allowing you to learn at your own pace; and
- videos on HMRC's YouTube pages.

## Records

It is strongly recommended that a separate bank account is maintained for all business income, purchases and expenses. As a minimum you should keep the following records, either electronically or manually:

- a cash book to record and analyse sales and other receipts, purchases and overhead expenses that pass through the bank account; and
- a petty cash book to log all small transactions paid for in cash.

If you run a larger business, you will probably need to maintain other accounting information as well.

> ### Tax Saver
>
> Whatever the size of your business it is a good discipline to:
>
> - write up all your books of account on a regular basis; and
> - maintain proper and accurate accounting records at all times.

Furthermore, in order to comply with the requirements for Self Assessment, you should keep and file the following:

- invoices for sales made by your business;
- bank statements and paying-in slips to show where the income comes from;
- invoices for goods acquired or costs incurred;
- documentation supporting purchases and sales of assets used in your business; and
- records in support of amounts taken out of the business for personal use (drawings) and all money paid into your business from personal funds (capital introduced).

# Accounts

When you draw up your accounts, you need to know what your accounting period is.

New businesses starting in 2024/25 will use the normal tax year to 5 April. Previously businesses have been able to select their own accounting period.

This is changing due to a switch from accruals based accounting to cash-based accounting for these unincorporated businesses.

## Cash v accruals

Under cash-basis accounting, you only record transactions when there is an actual inflow or outflow of cash. This means revenue is recorded at the time of cash receipt.

Accruals-based accounting recognizes transactions incurred or earned, regardless of when the cash is received or paid. Businesses that calculate their tax year using the cash basis will always calculate their taxes for the tax year beginning on 6 April.

Using the cash basis, businesses don't have to make any adjustment for:

- stocks or work in progress;
- unpaid bills for either purchases or overhead expenses; or
- outstanding invoices due from customers.

Until recently businesses calculating their taxes on an accruals basis have been able to choose their own tax year.

From April 2024, cash-basis accounting has been the default for all unincorporated businesses. If you wish to continue with accruals-basis accounting, you'll have to opt out of the cash-basis default.

When it comes to expenses make sure you claim all the overhead costs.

### Tax Saver

If you are married or live with a partner and your spouse/partner helps you in the business by doing your accounts and acting as a part-time secretary or assistant, you can claim the salary paid to him/her as a business expense. You should pay a proper amount for these services. If this is his or her only job or income and the wage is less than £12,570 for the year, then there will be no tax or National Insurance to pay.

### Tax Saver

If you work from home you can claim a deduction for an appropriate proportion of the fixed costs of running your home, such as:

- mortgage interest;
- council tax;
- light, heat and household insurance;
- the rental of your landline telephone;
- broadband;
- general repairs and maintenance; and
- cleaning expenses.

In order to be eligible you must have a specific area in your home set aside as an office.

### Tax Saver

There will be some costs of your business, such as a car used both privately and for work, when it may be difficult to apportion the expenditure between the private and business elements. Where there is this overlap, include a note in the additional information section of the self-employed pages of your Tax Return, so your tax office can see how you have worked out the percentage of the expenditure chargeable to the business.

## Tax Saver

Finally, avoid using estimates for any business expenses. If they are challenged on enquiry from HMRC you will find it difficult to substantiate what you have claimed in your accounts.

---

Jack Wagstaff has been in business for many years running the newsagents and confectionery shop in his local high street. He has three part-time assistants to help him in the shop.

His wife, Emily, looks after all the records of the business, pays the suppliers and completes the quarterly VAT Returns.

Jack makes up his accounts to 31 March each year. The statement of his business income and the expenses incurred during the year to 31 March 2025 are as follows:

|  |  | £ | £ | £ |
|---|---|---|---|---|
| **Sales** | | | | 182,650 |
| Less: | Cost of sales | | | |
| | Stock of cards, sweets, stationery, cigarettes etc at start of year | | 2,680 | |
| | Purchases in the year | | 61,440 | |
| | | | 64,120 | |
| Less: | Stock at end of year | | 3,240 | 60,880 |
| **Gross profit** | | | | 121,770 |
| Less: | Overhead expenses | | | |
| | Wages of part-time assistants | 20,400 | | |

*(continued)*

*(Continued)*

|  |  |  |
|---|---:|---:|
| Wife's salary | 6,200 | 26,600 |
| Shop expenses |  |  |
|     Rent | 22,000 |  |
|     Business and Water Rates | 13,750 |  |
|     Light and Heat | 3,800 |  |
|     Insurance | 820 |  |
|     Cleaning | 1,560 |  |
|     Shop door repairs | 620 | 42,550 |
|     Printing, postage and stationery |  | 1,660 |
|     Shop telephone and fax |  | 1,790 |
| Computer costs |  | 860 |
| Entertaining |  | 220 |
| Accountancy |  | 1,340 |
| Legal fees re new lease |  | 1,260 |
| Car expenses |  |  |
|     Road Fund Licence and insurance | 720 |  |
|     Petrol and oil | 1,720 |  |
|     Repairs and servicing | 530 | 2,970 |
| Use of home as office (1/6 × £2,730) |  | 455 |
| Home telephone |  | 820 |
| Bank interest and charges |  | 1,140 |
| Staff welfare |  | 390 |
| Miscellaneous expenses |  | 240 | 82,295 |
| **Profit for the year** |  | 39,475 |

Nowadays, annual accounts of a business are often needed for reasons other than tax. For example, to verify income in support of an application for a mortgage, or by your bank manager when weighing up an application for a business loan or overdraft facility.

## Cash accounting for businesses

From the 2024/25 tax year, if you're a sole trader or partner, cash basis is the default way to work out your income and expenses when you file your Self Assessment.

You will need to keep records using cash basis unless you cannot use this basis or choose to use traditional accounting.

From 2024/25, the cash basis will become the default method, and businesses will need to opt-out if they wish to continue using the accrual basis.

> **Tax Saver**
>
> Losses incurred can be carried forward to be set against profits of future years. However, losses cannot be carried back or set off against other income. This restriction on tax relief for losses could be a significant disadvantage to some businesses.

## Fixed-rate deduction scheme

You can also use optional simplified flat rate calculations to work out some of your business expenses. The main types of expenditure covered are those relating to cars, vans or motorcycles, and the use of your home. For each vehicle the costs included in the fixed deduction cover both the purchase and all running costs. Once the fixed-rate scheme has been used for a vehicle it is compulsory for each subsequent period that the vehicle is used in the business. The allowable rates for 2024/25 are:

|  | For each of the first 10,000 business miles | For each business mile over 10,000 |
| --- | --- | --- |
| Cars and goods vehicles | 45 p | 25 p |
| Motorbikes | 24 p | 24 p |

For use of your home, you can deduct a fixed monthly rate which depends on the number of hours you, or any of your employees, spend working at your home. The monthly rates of deduction for 2024/25 are:

| Number of hours worked per month | Allowable amount |
|---|---|
| 25 to 50 | £10 |
| 51 to 100 | £18 |
| 101 or more | £26 |

However, this flat rate does not include the proportion of your telephone or internet used for your business. You can claim these expenses by working out the actual costs incurred.

## Small business income allowance

There is a tax-free allowance of £1,000 for individuals:

- whose income from selling goods or providing services is small; and
- which will provide certainty regarding the tax obligations for the growing number of 'micro-entrepreneurs' such as occasional eBay sellers.

There is no reporting requirement where gross income is below £1,000. If income exceeds this threshold you can choose to either:

- claim expenses in the usual way; or
- simply deduct the allowance from gross income and ignore expenses.

You can decide which method to adopt on a year-by-year basis.

## Tax Return information

If you were in business at any time during the 2024/25 tax year you will need to complete the supplementary self-employment pages to accompany your Tax Return for the year. The self-employment pages are in a set format for reporting the annual income and expenses of your business. Your Return will not be accepted as complete if the information about your business income and expenses is not presented in the required format.

When Jack Wagstaff comes to complete the supplementary self-employment pages for the year ended 5 April 2025 he will fill in the section on business income and expenses, based on his accounts for the financial year to 31 March 2025, as follows:

|  | £ |
|---|---:|
| **Sales/business income (excluding VAT)** | 182,650 |
| **Expenses** | |
| Cost of goods bought for re-sale or goods used | 60,880 |
| Payments to subcontractors | – |
| Wages, salaries and other staff costs | 26,600 |
| Car, van and travel expenses | 2,970 |
| Rent, rates, power and insurance costs | 40,825 |
| Repairs and renewals of property and equipment | 620 |
| Telephone, fax, stationery and other office costs | 5,830 |
| Advertising and business entertainment costs | 220 |
| Interest on bank and other loans | 1,140 |
| Bank, credit card and other financial charges | – |
| Irrecoverable debts written off | – |
| Accountancy, legal and other professional fees | 2,600 |
| Other finance charges | – |
| Depreciation and loss/(profit) on sale of assets | – |
| Other business expenses | 1,490 |
| **Total expenses** | 143,175 |
| **Net profit** | 39,475 |
| **Notes** | |
| *(1) Wages, salaries and other staff costs* | |
|     Part-time assistants | 20,400 |
|     Wife's salary | 6,200 |
| | 26,600 |
| *(2) Rent rates, power and insurance costs* | |
|     Shop expenses (excluding cleaning and door repairs) | 40,370 |
|     Use of home as office | 455 |
| | 40,825 |

*(continued)*

*(Continued)*

| | |
|---|---:|
| *(3) Telephone, fax, stationery and other office costs* | |
| Printing, postage and stationery | 1,660 |
| Telephone (shop and home) | 2,610 |
| Shop cleaning | 1,560 |
| | 5,830 |
| *(4) Accountancy, legal and other professional costs* | |
| Accountancy | 1,340 |
| Legal fees | 1,260 |
| | 2,600 |
| *(5) Other business expenses* | |
| Computer costs | 860 |
| Staff welfare | 390 |
| Miscellaneous expenses | 240 |
| | 1,490 |

So as to minimize the risk of HMRC raising enquiries into your self-employment income and Tax Return, you should adopt a consistent pattern from year to year in the way you analyse your business expenses under the various headings of the standardized format.

If the annual turnover of your business was below £90,000:

- you only need to complete the self-employment (short) supplementary pages; and
- you can add up all your business expenses allowable for tax purposes and just enter the total figure in Box 20 on page SES1.

# Profits for tax

The profit disclosed by your business accounts will not necessarily be the same as that on which your tax bill is calculated. This is because certain types of expenditure are specifically not allowable in working out taxable business profits. These include:

- goods or materials bought for personal use;
- the private proportion of mixed expenses;
- business entertainment;

- non-business charitable donations;
- amounts spent on items of a capital nature;
- professional costs related to capital expenditure;
- own wages or drawings; and
- general provisions and reserves.

---

Although Jack Wagstaff's accounts for his financial year to 31 March 2025 show he made a profit of £39,475, his taxable profit is £43,311 as follows:

|  | £ | £ |
|---|---|---|
| Profit as per accounts |  | 39,475 |
| *Add*: Disallowable expenses |  |  |
| Private proportion of car expenses (60 per cent) | 1,782 |  |
| Private proportion of home telephone (70 per cent) | 574 |  |
| Entertainment | 220 |  |
| Legal fees re new lease | 1,260 |  |
|  |  | 3,809 |
| Profit as adjusted for tax purposes |  | 43,284 |

---

# Pre-trading and post-cessation expenses

Any expenditure which you incurred in the seven years before you started to trade is treated as if it was spent on the first day of business, and tax deductible.

The relief only extends to those costs and other outgoings which would qualify for tax relief had they been incurred on the first day of trading.

Tax relief is also allowed on certain expenditure incurred after your business has ceased. The expenses that qualify for relief are:

- those closely related to the trading or professional activities previously carried on; and
- including, for example, relief for debts that have subsequently proved to be irrecoverable.

Relief is available for payments made within seven years of the permanent discontinuance of the business by setting the payments made against income for the same tax year. Any excess can be treated as a capital loss, but only of the same tax year.

# Capital allowances

Businesses that pay Corporation Tax can claim what are known as capital allowances on the expenditure they incur on capital items. These include items such as manufacturing and IT equipment. The relief is now very generous and is known as 'full expensing'. In other words, the full value of the equipment can be used to reduce the tax bill.

Let's imagine a business starts with a £1 million Corporation Tax bill. If it spends £2 million on new equipment in one year, the company would reduce its tax liability by £500,000. (The current rate of Corporation Tax is 25 per cent.)

# Losses

It is almost inevitable that your business will go through both good and bad times. If so, you need to be aware of, and to consider, all of the different options for claiming the tax relief due on the loss.

> **Tax Saver**
>
> If you incur a loss you can claim tax relief on the loss sustained as increased by the amount of your capital allowances for the same period. You can choose whether to set a trading loss against other income in either the same, or the preceding, tax year. But you cannot claim to relieve only part of a loss.

> Isabel Fletcher has been in business for many years. She makes up her accounts to 5 April each year. In the year ended 5 April 2024 she makes a loss that she can claim against her other income in 2024/25. Alternatively, the loss can be carried back and relieved against her total income in 2023/24.

Any unrelieved loss of your business then has to be carried forward for off-set against profits from the same business in future years.

Alternatively you can claim to set a trading loss against capital gains (see Chapter 13) in the following way.

- The claim is for relief on the amount of the trading loss that cannot be set against your other income in the year or on which tax relief has already been given in some other way.
- The maximum loss eligible for relief against capital gains is the same as the amount of your gains chargeable to Capital Gains Tax.

It is not possible to make a partial claim.

> **Tax Saver**
>
> By relieving a business loss this way you may be wasting personal allowances as well as your annual exemption for Capital Gains.

Tax relief for losses incurred by new businesses is extended such that:

- losses incurred during the first four tax years can be set against your total income for the three years prior to that in which the loss arises; and
- relief is first of all given against total income for the earliest year.

There is one final type of loss relief that is only available to those businesses that incur a loss in their last period of trading. In such circumstances there cannot be future profits against which such a loss might be relieved. Therefore, a loss arising in the last 12 months of trading can be set back against the profits from the same business in both the final and three preceding tax years, beginning with the profits of the last year and working backwards.

> Ralph Collins retires from business on **30 September 2024**. In the final nine months in business he loses £18,000. Previously his business had always been successful as follows:
>
> | Accounting year | Taxable profits (£) | Year of charge |
> |---|---|---|
> | Year ended 31 December 2020 | 16,000 | 2018/19 |
>
> *(continued)*

(Continued)

| Accounting year | Taxable profits (£) | Year of charge |
|---|---|---|
| Year ended 31 December 2021 | 12,000 | 2019/20 |
| Year ended 31 December 2022 | 9,000 | 2020/21 |
| Year ended 31 December 2023 | 4,000 | 2021/22 |

The terminal loss can be set off as follows:

| | | |
|---|---|---|
| 2023/24 | £4,000 | leaving nil taxable profits |
| 2022/23 | £9,000 | leaving nil taxable profits |
| 2021/22 | £5,000 | reducing the taxable profits to £7,000 |
| | £18,000 | |

# Limit of reliefs

There is a limit on the amount of certain Income Tax reliefs that you can claim. This annual 'cap' is the greater limit of £50,000 or 25 per cent of your total income.

The reliefs caught by this rule include:

- claiming to set off early year, annual or post-cessation trading losses against other income, but not capital gains; and
- qualifying loan interest (see Chapter 4).

In 2024/25 Ben Turner suffered a loss of £60,000 in his business. Ben made a claim to offset this loss against his total income for the year of £140,000. The maximum loss that can be relieved is £50,000 as this is more than £35,000 (25 per cent of Ben's income of £140,000).

The restriction of relief for business losses may have a significant adverse impact on the finances of owners of any small- or medium-sized businesses:

- suffering a blip in profitability; or

- investing in plant or machinery to take advantage of the Annual Investment Limit.

## Taking on staff

You have now reached the time where your business is expanding. You need an assistant or an extra pair of hands. When you start employing staff you need to register as an employer with HMRC before the first payday.

As an employer, you are responsible for several things.

- Working out the deductions for Income Tax (PAYE) and National Insurance Contributions from the salary or wage paid to your employees at regular weekly or monthly intervals.
- Paying over the deductions to the Collector of Taxes each month. These payments can be made every quarter where your average monthly payments of PAYE and National Insurance Contributions are less than £1,500.
- Letting your tax office know every year how much each employee has earned together with the deductions made for both Income Tax and National Insurance Contributions. The deductions should reconcile to the total of the amounts paid over to the Collector of Taxes. You must also give details of any benefits paid or provided.
- Giving your employees certificates showing their earnings for the tax year, deductions for Income Tax and National Insurance Contributions and the value of any benefits provided.

## Some other ways to save on tax

> ### Tax Saver
>
> Look into taking your spouse/partner into partnership where he or she helps you in the business and your annual profits are such that the top slice is taxable at the higher **40 per cent** or additional **45 per cent** rates. Between you it may be possible to make significant savings in your overall annual tax bill.

> **Tax Saver**
>
> If your business is growing and becoming ever more profitable you should seriously think about transferring it to a limited company with the following advantages.
>
> - The rate of tax paid by a company on its profits is much lower than the corresponding Income Tax rates on personal income.
> - The members' liability is limited to the amount paid for their shares and any loans to the company.
> - Once formed a company can exist forever.
> - No other person can use the company name.
> - New shareholders and investors can easily be introduced.
>
> Finally, when you want to retire it is far easier to:
>
> - sell your stake in a company; or
> - transfer ownership of your shares,
>
> than sell, or pass on, a business operating as a sole trader.

> **Tax Saver**
>
> Finally, always look to the future and plan for your retirement, whether you are contemplating a sale of your business or handing it down to the next generation.

# Foster carers

Those who receive income from local authorities or independent fostering providers for providing foster care to children and young people, or are qualified shared-lives carers, are entitled to a special relief, which comes in two parts:

- an exemption from Income Tax on receipts that do not exceed the qualifying amount for any year; and

- a simplified optional method of calculating taxable profits where receipts are more than the qualifying amount.

The annual qualifying amount is made up of two parts, which must be added together. They are:

- a fixed amount for each household – £19,360 for 2024/25; and
- a weekly amount for each foster child placed with you – this varies by age; for 2024/25 the allowance is £405 for children under 11, £485 for children aged 11 and over.

Where your receipts (fees, salaries, reward payments, allowances, etc) exceed the annual qualifying amount you can choose between paying tax on:

- your actual profits from foster caring, worked out on the principles that apply for any other business; or
- profits worked out on a simplified method, which is the difference between your total receipts for the year less the annual qualifying amount.

Whichever way you choose to be taxed you must at least keep records of your receipts and the ages and number of weeks that you care for each child placed with you. For this purpose a week runs from Monday to the following Sunday. Part of a week counts as a full week.

# Furnished holiday accommodation

The furnished holiday accommodation tax regime is soon to be abolished from 6 April 2025 for Income Tax and Capital Gains Tax (and from 1 April 2025 for Corporation Tax). This was part of the chancellor's Autumn Budget 2024 speech given in October of that year.

However, it is worth briefly giving an overview of this for anyone who can still take advantage before its abolishment.

The letting of furnished holiday accommodation in both the United Kingdom and anywhere else in the European Economic Area may be treated as a trade as long as the property is:

- let commercially and furnished;
- available for letting commercially to the public as holiday accommodation for at least 210 days in a 12-month period; and
- actually let for at least 105 such days.

Any period exceeding 31 days during which the property is occupied by the same person does not count towards the 105 days test.

If, in any 12-month period, the periods of occupation of more than 31 days total more than 155 days the accommodation will not qualify under these rules.

## Other special situations

So far, only a general picture of the way in which the profits of most businesses are taxed has been put forward. If you are a farmer, a writer, a Lloyds underwriter or a subcontractor in the construction industry, you should know that there are special rules for working out the taxable profits from these and some other trades, professions or vocations. In such situations it is advisable to seek professional assistance.

# 08
# National Insurance and state benefits

Employed or self-employed, you must pay National Insurance Contributions as well as Income Tax on your earnings or business profits. By paying sufficient National Insurance Contributions you become eligible to claim those social security benefits that are based on your contribution history. Many benefits, mainly those payable to the disabled, do not depend upon the payment of contributions.

## National Insurance numbers

You need to have a National Insurance number (NINO) so that all the contributions you make can be properly recorded. It is unique to you and made up of two letters and six numbers, followed by a further letter – A, B, C or D. You keep the same number for your whole life.

All children are notified of their NINO shortly before their 16th birthday providing they live in the UK and their parents or guardians are receiving Child Benefit for them.

Or you can apply at any time over the age of 16:

- in order to claim tax credits and/or benefits;
- when you start in employment or working for yourself; or
- if you have applied for a student loan.

If any of these circumstances apply, and you are under 20 years old, you should contact the National Insurance Registrations Helpline on 0300 200 3500. Otherwise, you should call the National Insurance number application line on 0800 141 2075.

# National Insurance Contributions

There are four classes of contribution payable as follows:

- Class 1 by employees and employers;
- Class 2 for the self-employed which are now voluntary;
- Class 3 which is voluntary; and
- Class 4 by the self-employed, based on profits of your business.

The rates of National Insurance Contributions for 2024/25 are listed in Appendix 3.

At the present time there is a gradual increase in State Pension Age for both men and women to:

- age 66; then
- to 67 and 68,

depending on when you were born.

You do not have to go on paying contributions once you attain State Pension age, even if you carry on working either:

- in employment; or
- for yourself in your own business.

## (a) Class 1

The earnings of employees on which contributions are calculated include:

- a salary or wage – before deduction for pension contributions;
- overtime, bonuses and commission;
- holiday pay; and
- Statutory Sick, Maternity and Paternity Pay.

No contributions are payable by employees on:

- business expenses;
- tips and gratuities; or
- redundancy payments.

The contributions you pay are usually a percentage of your weekly or monthly salary or wage, subject to lower and upper-earnings limits that change from year to year. The rate and amount of contribution you pay when you return to work is unaffected if you change jobs and have a break between them, or there is a period when you are unemployed.

Employers also pay Class 1 National Insurance Contributions, based on how much the employee earns.

We'll break down the rates comprehensively in Appendix 3, but in 2024/25 employee rates can range from 1.85 per cent to 8 per cent. Meanwhile, employer rates are typically 13.8 per cent but this will rise after the end of the tax year.

> **Tax Saver**
>
> If you have more than one employment you must pay contributions on your earnings from all your jobs. However, there is an overall annual maximum limit of contributions payable by employees. You can apply for a refund in any year where the total contributions you have paid exceed this annual limit. Alternatively, by completing form **CA72A**, you can apply for deferment where you reckon that the contributions you will pay on earnings from two or more employments will exceed the maximum annual limit.
>
> The National Insurance Contributions and Employer Office of HMRC will then instruct one or other of your employers not to withhold contributions from your earnings. After the end of the tax year your overall contribution history is reviewed. If you have not paid enough contributions the National Insurance Contributions Office will send you a calculation and a demand for the balance due.

## (b) Class 2

Scrapped in April 2024, self-employed workers used to have to pay Class 2 contributions. However, this is no longer the case, though if a self-employed person's profits are more than £12,570 a year they must pay Class 4 contributions.

However, it is worth noting if you are self-employed you can choose to pay Class 2 contributions to cover any gaps in your National Insurance record.

## (c) Class 3

The payment of these flat-rate contributions is voluntary. It may sometimes be beneficial to pay Class 3 contributions, such as when you have been:

- in a job but your wage was below the lower earnings limit;
- abroad; or
- in prison.

Ask HMRC to check your National Insurance Record. They will be able to tell you if you can make these voluntary contributions, and how much you can pay.

By doing so you fill in gaps in your contribution history. This will help in satisfying the requirement for benefits such as the State Pension. You can usually only pay for gaps in your National Insurance record for the last six years.

## (d) Class 4

These are payable by the self-employed based on a percentage of taxable business profits, after capital allowances, but before relief for pension contributions. They are paid each year through Self Assessment along with the Income Tax due on business profits. The 2024/25 rates are 6 per cent on profits between £12,570 and £50,270, and 2 per cent on profits above the latter.

# Social Security benefits

Responsibility for administering all aspects of the Social Security system lies with the Department for Work and Pensions (DWP). There are local DWP offices all across the country. The framework of the Social Security system is now so substantial, and the range of benefits so wide and varied, that it is only possible for me to give a brief summary of the main state benefits and benefit categories.

- Universal Credit, the main benefit for people of working age on low income, replaces three benefits and three tax credits (some claimants are still receiving the predecessor benefits or credits).
- Working-age benefits (for those under pension age), administered by Jobcentre Plus.
- Pension-age benefits (for those of pension age and over), administered by the Pension, Disability and Carers Service.

- Child Benefit for families with children and people in work, administered by HMRC.
- Disability and carer benefits, administered by the Department of Work and Pensions.

Some but not all benefits are only available to claimants who have paid sufficient National Insurance Contributions.

## (a) Statutory Sick Pay

To be able to claim Statutory Sick Pay you must be paying sufficient Class 1 contributions. There are also several other points to remember.

- It is a flat-rate cash payment made to employees by their employer.
- To claim you must be both incapable of work and not actually do any work at all on the day in question.
- It is not payable for the first three agreed qualifying days in any period when you are too unwell to work.
- In any period of sickness you have a maximum entitlement to 28 weeks of Statutory Sick Pay.

## (b) Statutory Maternity Pay

Eligibility for Statutory Maternity Pay is again dependent on the payment of Class 1 contributions, as well as other measures.

- A woman qualifies for Statutory Maternity Pay if she has been working continuously for the same employer for 26 weeks up to, and including, the 15th week before her baby is due.
- A woman must provide evidence of being pregnant and give her employer sufficient notice of leaving work.
- She will receive benefit for 39 weeks beginning not earlier than the 11th week before the baby is due, although she can actually select the time over which she will be absent from work.

## (c) Statutory Paternity Pay

The basic features of ordinary Statutory Paternity Pay are:

- fathers are allowed up to two weeks away from work during the first eight weeks of their child's life;

- it is also a flat-rate cash payment; and
- the qualifying requirements are the same as those for Statutory Maternity Pay.

## (d) Shared Parental Leave and Pay

As the name implies, the purpose behind these benefits is to allow eligible couples to swap the role of the main carer of their child between them.

You can either be having a baby, or adopting a child.

You can go to the government website to find out:

- if you can get Maternity, Paternity or Shared Parental Leave; and
- how much you will receive if you take leave.

## (e) Universal Credit

Universal Credit replaces six previous benefits and tax credits:

1. CTC
2. Housing Benefit
3. Income Support
4. Income-based Jobseekers Allowance (JSA)
5. Income-related Employment & Support Allowance (ESA)
6. WTC

The Credit is designed to help people with their living costs. People on a low income or who are out of work, or unable to work, may be able to claim. If you're still receiving one of the six predecessor benefits or credits, you will soon receive a 'migration notice' to move you over to Universal Credit.

### Eligibility for Universal Credit

To claim you must:

- live in the UK;
- be aged 18 or over (there are some exceptions if you're 16 or 17);
- be under State Pension Age;
- have no more than £16,000 in cash, savings or investments.

If you live with a partner, you will both need to claim for Universal Credit. You must make a joint claim for your household even if your partner is not eligible. The amount of credit you will receive will depend on your partner's income and savings, as well as your own.

If only one of you has reached State Pension age, you can still claim Universal Credit as part of a couple. Your Universal Credit claim will stop when you reach State Pension Age.

## *(f) Child Benefit*

Child Benefit is payable:

- to individuals bringing up children;
- for all children under 16 years old; and
- for children between 16 and 20 if they stay in approved education or training.

It is not means-tested and for couples who are married it is the mother who should make the claim.

High-income claimants receiving Child Benefit:

- are subject to a tax charge (see Chapter 11); but
- can opt not to receive the benefit if they or their spouse/partner want to avoid paying the charge.

### Weekly Child Benefit rates

| Rates (£ per week) | 2024 to 2025 |
| --- | --- |
| Eldest or only child | £25.60 |
| Other children | £16.95 |

### Tax Saver

Electing not to receive Child Benefit, in order to avoid the High Income Child Benefit Charge (see Chapter 11), is not the same as not making a claim in the first instance. A claim should always be made and then followed by the

> opt out. This ensures the claimant, usually the mother, is credited with National Insurance Contributions. As a result entitlement to the State Pension or other benefits is not jeopardized.

### (g) Personal Independence Payment

To be eligible for a Personal Independence Payment (PIP) you must:

- be aged 16 to 64;
- have a long-term health condition or disability; and
- have difficulties with daily living activities or mobility.

PIP is tax-free and comprises standard and enhanced components for both the daily living and mobility components.

You can get PIP even if you're working, have savings, or are getting other benefits. Gradually PIP is replacing the Disability Living Allowance currently paid to claimants of that allowance. However, the Disability Living Allowance continues if:

- you're under 16; or
- you were born on or before 8 April 1948.

### (h) Attendance Allowance

Attendance Allowance is paid to people over the age of 65 who:

- are seriously disabled, mentally or physically; and
- need a lot of care and attention both throughout the day and at night.

## Capital limits

If your capital is over £16,000, you will not be entitled to:

- Universal Credit;
- Income Support;

- Housing Benefit; or
- JSA and ESA.

The amount of the above benefits you will receive is tapered where your capital is between £6,000 and £16,000. Capital includes:

- cash;
- funds held in a bank or building society account; and
- shares or investment trusts at market value or surrender rate less 10 per cent.

# Cap on benefits

The maximum weekly amount that individuals can receive in benefits depends on where they live. For 2024/25, the figures are as follows:

| Claimant | Inside Greater London (£) | Outside Greater London (£) |
|---|---|---|
| Single adult households without children | 326.29 | 283.71 |
| Couples (with or without children) or single claimants with a child of qualifying age | 486.98 | 423.46 |

The 'cap' applies to the combined amounts of:

- Universal Credit;
- Incapacity Benefit;
- JSA;
- Income Support;
- ESA;
- Housing Benefit;
- Child Benefit;
- CTC;
- Universal Credit; and
- Bereavement, Widowed Parents, Maternity and Severe Disablement Allowances.

Some households including those with someone receiving:

- PIP;
- Disability Living Allowance;
- Carer's or Guardian's Allowances;
- Attendance Allowance; or
- the Support component of the ESA,

are exempt, as are war widows, widowers and households with someone entitled to the WTC.

## Benefits and rates

Listed in Appendix 4 are all the Social Security benefits, distinguishing between those that are taxable and non-taxable.

Following on is Appendix 5, which gives the rates of the main Social Security benefits for 2024/25.

## State Pension Credit

An individual is entitled to the State Pension Credit if he or she:

- lives in Great Britain;
- satisfies at least one of two requirements of the guarantee and savings credits respectively; and
- has reached the qualifying age.

> **Tax Saver**
>
> The guarantee credit 'tops up' your weekly income to £218.15 per week if you're single for 2024/25, and to £332.95 jointly if you have a partner.

A claimant's income includes:

- a state and any other pension;
- earnings;

- some Social Security benefits; and
- notional investment income of £1 a week for every £500 of savings or capital in excess of £10,000 (excluding your home and possessions).

The purpose of the savings credit, the rules for which are far from simple, is to reduce Pension Credit by 40 per cent of the amount by which a pensioner's income exceeds the appropriate minimum guarantee.

The guarantee credit is available to:

- both men and women who have reached the State Pension age for women; and
- a member of a couple where the other partner has attained the State Pension age for women.

The qualifying age for both men and women increases to age 65 for the savings credit element.

# 09
# State and private pensions

I don't doubt that when you give up work and retire you will want to be able to maintain your lifestyle and living standards. You may have built up savings while you were working, but your income in retirement is most likely to come from:

- the State Pension; and
- an employer or personal pension scheme.

So that you can give yourself the best possible opportunity to build up a good pension, you should start contributing to a plan as soon as you can reasonably afford to do so.

## The new State Pension

If you attained the State Pension age after 5 April 2016 you are eligible for the new State Pension.

The full new State Pension is £221.20 per week. However, there are several important things to remember about the new State Pension.

- Your National Insurance record is used to work out how much you will actually receive.
- You usually need at least 10 qualifying years before you are entitled to any new State Pension.
- To get the full new State Pension you must have 35 qualifying years.
- You may be able to pay Voluntary National Insurance Contributions if you have gaps in your contribution history that would stop you getting the full pension.

You may get credits towards your National Insurance Contributions record if you are a carer, unemployed or cannot work because of a disability or illness.

You should receive a letter, about four months before you reach your State Pension age, telling you what to do and how to make your claim. You can do this online, over the phone or by downloading the State Pension claim form.

If you are widowed you might be able to inherit an extra payment in addition to your new State Pension. But this will not apply if you remarry or form a civil partnership before you attain State Pension age.

## Deferment

You don't have to take your State Pension when you reach retirement age. If you defer taking your pension, you can boost your income when you do finally take the pension.

If you reach (or reached) your State Pension age on or after 6 April 2016, your State Pension will increase every week you defer, as long as you defer for at least nine weeks.

Your State Pension increases by the equivalent of 1 per cent for every nine weeks you defer. The State Pension is liable to Income Tax and this applies to an increased weekly pension.

If you reached pension age before 6 April 2016, you could either receive an increased weekly payment when you take your pension, or be paid a lump sum.

The lump sum is taxed at your marginal rate of Income Tax. You can elect for it to be paid and then be taxed in the following year.

## State Pension forecast

As you approach retirement age, for State Pension purposes it is a good idea to get a forecast of what you will receive from the DWP.

You can get a State Pension forecast if you are more than 30 days away from State Pension age when your application is processed. Your forecast will advise you in today's money of how much State Pension you may get, and the number of qualifying years on your National Insurance record.

The application form BR19 is available from the Pension Service by telephoning 0800 731 0175. Alternatively, the forecast can be obtained online.

# Private pensions

There are a number of attractions in saving for your retirement through a private pension plan. If you are self-employed you will need to make your own arrangements. For those of you working in employment your employer will be running a scheme for the employees of the business that you can join.

> **Tax Saver**
>
> The main features of pension provision are as follows.
>
> - You receive full tax relief on your allowable premiums.
> - Your contributions are invested in a tax-free fund.
> - You can take your benefits from the age of 55.
> - You do not have to retire to access your benefits.

## *(a) Annual contributions*

You can get tax relief on the payment of pension contributions:

- up to 100 per cent of your annual earnings; but
- subject to a maximum annual allowance, which is £60,000.

The maximum annual allowance was £40,000 prior to 2023/24. However, the allowance is:

- reduced by £1 for every £2 of your net income above £260,000; and
- reduced to £4,000 when your income is £360,000 or more.

Furthermore, once you start drawing taxable income from your pension fund you are also restricted to paying pension contributions not exceeding £10,000 each year.

The annual allowance:

- does not set a limit on pension contributions in a tax year; but

- is by reference to the 'pension input period' for each pension scheme ending in a tax year.

In calculating how much has been contributed you need to take into account:

- payments into all your pension schemes ending in the tax year; and
- any employer contributions.

If more than the annual allowance is contributed, the excess is taxed at your marginal rate of tax.

## (b) Unused allowances

If your contributions exceed the annual allowance in a tax year, you will not be liable to the excess charge providing you have sufficient unused allowances brought forward from the three previous years.

Contributions are first of all allocated to the annual allowance for the current year. Any excess can then be set against any unused allowances brought forward. Those of an earlier year are used first.

---

Warren Baker is employed as a senior manager on a salary of £50,000 per annum. He is a member of his employer's pension scheme, which has a pension input period running from each 1 April to the following 31 March. The company contributes 10 per cent of Warren's salary towards his pension. He pays in 6 per cent of his salary. The contributions each year from Warren and his employer total £8,000.

In June 2024 Warren is awarded a bonus of £100,000 by his employer for securing a valuable long-term contract for the company.

Warren decides to pay £80,000 from the bonus into his pension as a one-off extra contribution. Warren's pension input amount in 2024/25 of £88,000 (£80,000 + £8,000) exceeds his annual allowance by £48,000. However, he has unused annual allowances brought forward from previous years as follows:

|         | Unused allowances brought forward (£) | Utilized in 2024/25 (£) | Carried forward (£) |
|---------|---------------------------------------|-------------------------|---------------------|
| 2024/25 | 34,000                                | –                       | 34,000              |
| 2023/24 | 32,000                                | 16,000                  | 16,000              |
| 2022/23 | 32,000                                | 32,000                  | –                   |
|         |                                       | 48,000                  |                     |

First of all Warren uses up his unused allowance from 2022/23. This is followed by £16,000 from 2023/24 leaving unused allowances from 2022/23 and 2023/24 totalling £48,000 to carry forward to 2024/25.

## (c) Drawing your pension from age 55

### Tax Saver

Until you dip into your pension fund it is called an uncrystallized fund. Twenty-five per cent of any lump sums taken out of the fund are tax-free; the balance is taxed as income.

But once you start taking a regular income by:

- going into a regular drawdown plan; or
- purchasing an annuity,

only the first withdrawal of 25 per cent, or less, of the full value is free of tax.

In 2024/25 John Hill has earnings of £25,000. His tax bill, all at 20 per cent, is £2,486. His pension pot is £200,000 and he decides to take half of it. 25 per cent of the £100,000 withdrawal is tax-free leaving £75,000 taxable. His tax liability for 2024/25 increases to £27,432 as follows:

|  | £ |
|---|---|
| Taxable pension fund withdrawal | 75,000 |
| Earnings | 25,000 |
|  | 100,000 |
| *Less*: Personal allowance | 12,570 |
| Taxable income | 87,430 |
| Income Tax payable |  |
| £37,700 @ 20 per cent | 7,540 |
| £49,730 @ 40 per cent | 19,892 |
|  | 27,432 |

Tax at source under the PAYE system is taken off by your pension provider on both:

- lump sum payments; and
- regular income,

drawn from your pension pot.

As it is more than likely that too much tax will be deducted from lump sum withdrawals, the following forms are available from HMRC to reclaim any tax overpayment. These are:

- Form P50Z, which is used if you have cashed in your entire pension fund and you have no other income in the year;
- Form P53, which is relevant if you have withdrawn all your pension pot but you do have other taxable income in the year; and
- Form P55, which applies when you make a partial withdrawal but no further cash withdrawals are intended in the same tax year.

Savers who are thinking about taking money from their pension funds can access free guidance so they can better understand their retirement income options under these rules. This is available from either:

- Pension Wise, a free service set up by the government; or
- The Citizens Advice Bureau.

## (d) Death benefits

On death, special rules apply to funds held in a pension pot because Inheritance Tax (see Chapter 17) is not usually charged on money held in a pension.

> ### Tax Saver
>
> If you die before age 75 and leave funds in a defined contribution pension fund your nominated beneficiaries can inherit the fund tax-free. This applies whether they:
>
> - take one or more lump sum withdrawals; or
> - use the fund for income.
>
> However, from 6 April 2027 a person's unused pension will no longer be exempt from Inheritance Tax and therefore be included in someone's estate.

But if you are over 75 years old when you die, a beneficiary who opts for:

- a lump sum; or
- regular amounts,

will pay Income Tax at his or her marginal rate on what they receive.

# 10
# Savings and investment income

There are likely to be occasions during your lifetime when you will be:

- making regular savings out of income;
- investing a lump sum from a pension scheme on retirement; or
- in receipt of a much more substantial sum such as an inheritance or, perhaps, winnings on the National Lottery.

Examples of savings and investment income are:

- bank or building society interest;
- share and unit trust dividends;
- rents;
- interest on government stocks; and
- income from a trust fund.

## Tax-free income

> ### Tax Saver
>
> The most widely known investments where the return is tax-free are some of those available from National Savings and Investments. Individuals in the top tax brackets should take a look at them. They are:
>
> - Fixed-Interest and Index-Linked Savings Certificates*; and
> - Premium Bond Prizes.
>
> *Although no issues are on general sale at the time of writing, the total value of any maturing certificates can be renewed.
>
> Since 1 May 2019 National Savings & Investments (NS&I) have changed the inflation measure they use to calculate returns on their index-linked savings certificates from the Retail Price Index (RPI) to the Consumer Price Index (CPI).

Also tax-free are:

- interest on cash ISAs;
- dividends from ISA investments; and
- dividends paid on shares in Venture Capital Trusts.

Tax-free income does not need to be reported on your annual Income Tax Return.

## Savings income

Savings income is that such as interest on:

- bank/building society accounts;
- British Government stocks;
- National Savings Guaranteed Growth and Income Bonds, Savings and Investment accounts; and
- any other interest-bearing accounts or funds.

You will:

- receive your interest without any deduction for tax; and
- may also get up to £1,000 of tax-free interest depending on which tax bracket you are in.

Known as the Personal Savings Allowance, the amounts of tax-free savings income for 2024/25 are as follows:

| Type of taxpayer | Amount of tax-free savings income (£) |
| --- | --- |
| Basic rate | 1,000 |
| Higher rate | 500 |
| Additional rate | Nil |

Furthermore, a zero rate applies to the first £5,000 of taxable savings income. But this zero rate is only available on any part of your taxable savings income:

- of up to £5,000; and
- after taking off your personal allowance.

> **Tax Saver**
>
> To get all the interest on your savings income tax-free in 2024/25, your taxable income for the year should usually not exceed £18,570, comprising:
>
> - your personal allowance of £12,570;
> - the Personal Savings Allowance of £1,000;
> - plus £5,000.
>
> But it can be more if you are entitled to other allowances, such as:
>
> - the relief given to a registered blind person;
> - the married couple's allowance; and
> - the new transferable marriage tax allowance.

However, because earnings and pensions are treated as the first slice of taxable income, many taxpayers will not benefit from this nil tax rate on the first £5,000 of taxable savings income.

# Dividend income

For 2024/25:

- the nil rate band on dividend income is £500; and
- the rates of tax payable on dividends above the allowance stay as follows:

| For dividends otherwise taxable at | Rate (%) |
|---|---|
| Basic rate | 8.75 |
| Higher rate | 33.75 |
| Additional rate | 39.35 |

## Accrued income

Interest on fixed-rate investments is regarded as accruing from day-to-day between payment dates. While there are no tax implications on the transfer of assets between spouses or civil partners, accrued income transfers can sometimes be caught out. On a sale the vendor is charged Income Tax on the interest that has accrued from the previous payment date to the date of sale. The purchaser is allowed to deduct this amount from the interest received on the following payment date.

These arrangements cover both fixed and variable-rate stocks and bonds, including those issued by governments, companies and local authorities. But the arrangements will not affect you if the nominal value of your securities is under £5,000. Nominal value means the 'face value' of the bond – in other words, the amount that will be repaid to the bondholder on maturity.

---

The interest on a holding of 6 per cent Treasury Stock 2028 is payable on each 7 June and 7 December. The half-yearly interest on a holding of £30,000, sold for settlement on 15 August 2018, is £900.

$$\text{Accrued proportion} = \frac{69 \times £900}{183} = £339.34$$

---

## Rents

The letting of property, including isolated or casual lettings, is treated as a business for most tax purposes. This applies to any flat, house, shop or other property that you rent to tenants. Most of the rules for working out the taxable profits from a trade or profession are also relevant in working out your annual income from the letting of property. It follows, therefore, that if you are eligible you may want to adopt the cash accounting rules for businesses (see Chapter 7) in working out the taxable profit from your property letting activity.

Income from all your properties in the United Kingdom is pooled together, regardless of the type of lease.

However, unlike a trade or profession, losses from your property rental business can only be carried forward to be set against future profits from the same activities.

Other than expenditure of a capital nature, such as that on extensions, structural alterations or improvements, the general running costs of a property can be set against rental income. Included in allowable expenses are:

- fees incurred on letting out the property;
- rent collection and management costs;
- interest relating to your property letting business (see Chapter 4);
- replacing or repairing any items fixed to the property;
- replacing loose domestic items like carpets, curtains or other soft furnishings;
- general maintenance and redecorations;
- insurance premiums on buildings and contents policies;
- ground rent for leased premises;
- water rates and Council Tax;
- gardening, cleaning and security services; and
- your share of expenditure on the common parts of the let property.

As an alternative to claiming either capital allowances and actual expenses (such as fuel), you can opt for a fixed-rate deduction (see Chapter 7) for every mile you travel by car, motorcycle or goods vehicle on your property letting business. There is a tax-free allowance of £1,000 for individuals such as:

- Airbnb hosts; and
- those whose income from letting property is small.

The rules are the same as those which govern the small business income allowance.

Landlords had also been able to benefit from something called the Furnished Holiday Let (FHL) regime, meaning this income benefited from more beneficial capital allowance rules, access to reliefs and exemption from finance cost restriction. This was scrapped in the Autumn Budget 2024 and will cease from April 2025, whereupon income and gains from FHL will form part of someone's property business and be treated the same as other property assets.

> Karen Donnelly owns a flat that she let out to tenants during 2024/25. The net rental income for the year amounts to £14,090 as follows:
>
> |  | £ | £ |
> |---|---:|---:|
> | Rent receivable from the flat |  | 21,000 |
> | *Less*: Expenses |  |  |
> |   Agents fees for letting | 2,467 |  |
> |   Management fees | 740 |  |
> |   Ground rent | 200 |  |
> |   Service charges | 1,103 |  |
> |   Council tax for tenants | 960 |  |
> |   Water rates | 220 |  |
> |   Replacing bedroom curtains | 650 |  |
> |   Lounge redecoration | 490 |  |
> |   Boiler repair | 80 |  |
> |  |  | 6,910 |
> | £2024/25 net rental income |  | 14,090 |

# Rent-a-room

Income from the furnished letting of spare rooms in your home as residential accommodation is tax-free providing the gross rents do not exceed £7,500 per annum. The space you let out must be in your only or main home, which can be a house, flat, caravan or even a houseboat.

Where your annual gross rents are more than £7,500 you must elect if you want to pay tax on the excess gross rents, without any relief for expenses. If you do not do so then you will have to work out your taxable income using the rules for lettings income.

> Theresa Stevens is a basic-rate taxpayer who lets out spare rooms in her bungalow to lodgers paying £160 per week between them, £8,320 for 2024/25. The expenses that could be set against the lodgers' rents total £1,800 for the year.

> Theresa elects for rent-a-room relief and her Income Tax liability is £164 (£8,320 – £7,500) x 20 per cent. Under the normal rules her tax liability would come to £1,304 (£8,320 – £1,800) x 20 per cent.

The tax-free limit of £7,500 is halved where an individual and some other person are each entitled to income under the scheme. Each lessor's exempt amount is then £3,750.

### Tax Saver

You can elect to opt out of this special form of relief. It will benefit you to make the opt-out election if, for example, there is a loss on the letting that can be set against your other rental profits under the normal rules dealing with income from lettings.

### Tax Saver

If you need more income and do not want to move home, why not rent out a room to a lodger or bed-and-breakfast guest? Up to £7,500 a year (equivalent to a weekly rent of £144.20) is tax-free under this type of relief.

## Non-qualifying life policies

Most non-qualifying life policies are single premium life insurance policies. At the outset, a lump sum premium is paid into a bond that is, for example, either investment based or intended to produce a guaranteed income. An investor can usually:

- take regular amounts out;
- make ad hoc partial withdrawals; or
- leave the bond untouched until encashment or death, when it will form part of the investor's estate.

There is no tax relief on the single premium. Neither Capital Gains Tax nor Income Tax at the savings rate is payable on any profit. But investors whose income takes them into either the higher or additional rates of 40 per cent or 45 per cent will pay tax at the difference between their top rate and the basic rate of Income Tax on chargeable events. These arise on:

- surrender or maturity of the policy;
- death of the life assured; or
- withdrawals in excess of a cumulative allowance built up at the time.

At the end of each policy year an allowance of 5 per cent of the original investment is given. This applies on a cumulative basis so if not used can be carried forward from year to year. Over a period of 20 years, allowances of up to 100 per cent of the initial investment will be given. A taxable gain only arises if the amount of the withdrawal is more than the cumulative allowance at the time. Then it is the excess that is taxed.

In some cases, a wholly disproportionate liability to tax can arise on a part surrender. In such cases taxpayers can ask HMRC to recalculate historic charges on a just and reasonable basis. HMRC manuals advise that following a part surrender or part assignment of a life insurance policy, sections 507A and 512A allow an interested person to apply to an officer of HMRC to recalculate a gain on a just and reasonable basis. A recalculation will be performed on this basis if the officer decides that the gain is wholly disproportionate. The phrase 'wholly disproportionate' sets a high threshold. It is anticipated that there will be only very limited circumstances in which a gain will be regarded as wholly disproportionate and thus give rise to a recalculation.

When the final chargeable event on a bond occurs, the taxable gain is calculated by taking into account all previous withdrawals and taxable gains. In view of the wholly disproportionate tax charge that can arise from partial surrenders, most insurance companies sell bonds in segments which avoid the problem when fully surrendered golden rule, is that taxpayers can either restrict withdrawals to the 5 per cent cumulative limit allowed, or surrender complete segments.

---

Edward Clark invests £15,000 in an investment bond. Withdrawals of £600, £900 and £3,250 are made during the second, third and fifth policy years. The annual allowance is £750, being 5 per cent of the original investment. A taxable gain of £1,000 arises in year five as follows:

| Number of policy years | Cumulative allowance (£) | Amount withdrawn (£) | Cumulative withdrawal (£) | Taxable amount (£) |
|---|---|---|---|---|
| 1 | 750 | – | – | – |
| 2 | 1,500 | 600 | 600 | – |

| | | | | | |
|---|---|---|---|---|---|
| 3 | 2,250 | 900 | 1,500 | – | |
| 4 | 3,000 | – | 1,500 | – | |
| 5 | 3,750 | 3,250 | 4,750 | 1,000 | |

After seven years, Edward encashes the investment bond in the illustration above for £21,050. The taxable gain amounts to £9,800 as follows:

| | £ | £ |
|---|---|---|
| Policy proceeds | | 21,050 |
| *Add:* Withdrawals in years 2, 3 and 5 | | 4,750 |
| | | 25,800 |
| *Less:* | | |
| Original investment | 15,000 | |
| Amount already taxed | 1,000 | |
| | | 16,000 |
| Taxable gain on encashment | | 9,800 |

The method of calculating the Income Tax due on the taxable gain involves a number of stages, including 'top slicing' relief.

Edward is a single man. During 2024/25 his other income, all earnings, amounted to £45,850. He pays tax of £1,259.30 on the gain of £9,800 on the final encashment of his bond worked out as follows:

| | |
|---|---|
| Gain on encashment of bond | £9,800 |
| Number of years held | 7 |
| Taxable slice of gain | £1,400 |
| Taxable income – excluding slice of gain | |
| Earnings | £45,850 |
| *Less:* Personal allowance | £12,570 |
| | £33,280 |

| | |
|---|---:|
| Add slice of gain of £1,400 | £34,680 |
| *(below Income Tax basic rate allowance of £37,700, so top slice is all within basic rate band)* | |
| Average rate on slice | 0% |
| Tax payable on gain = £9,800 @ 0% | £0 |

> **Tax Saver**
>
> A non-qualifying life policy such as a single premium investment bond is a good way to supplement your income, particularly for anyone in the top tax brackets.

# Individual Savings Account

An Individual Savings Account (ISA) can include cash (including National Savings) or stocks and shares.

You do not pay any tax on the interest you earn in a cash ISA. Also free of tax are the income or capital profits in a stocks and shares ISA.

You can subscribe to an ISA if you are:

- both resident and ordinarily resident in the United Kingdom for tax purposes; and
- aged 18 or over, although 16- and 17-year-olds can invest just in cash.

> **Tax Saver**
>
> The annual subscription limit for all qualifying individuals:
>
> - is £20,000 in cash;
> - can be saved in just one type of account or split between both kinds.

> In May 2024 Lance Bishop put cash of £9,000 into a stocks and shares ISA. This left him with up to £11,000 available to invest in either a cash ISA or his stocks and shares ISA during the rest of 2024/25.

You can make withdrawals and then replace money in your cash ISA within the same tax year without these transactions counting towards your annual subscription limit.

> **Tax Saver**
>
> Spouses and civil partners can make an additional contribution to their ISAs equivalent to the value of their deceased spouses' or partners' ISAs at the date of death. You are allowed:
>
> - three years after the death of your spouse or civil partner; or
> - 180 days after the administration of the estate is complete, if later,
>
> in which to make this contribution which could result in significant savings in tax for the future.

Other features of an ISA are:

- there is no statutory lock-in period or minimum subscription;
- you can make withdrawals whenever you like; and
- there is no lifetime investment limit.

The list of investments that qualify for the stocks and shares component include:

- shares listed on a recognized Stock Exchange;
- shares quoted on the Alternative Investment Market;
- Unit Trusts;
- Investment Trusts;
- open-ended investment companies (OEIC); and
- government stocks with at least five years to go to maturity.

## Lifetime ISA

Taxpayers can also take out a Lifetime ISA into which:

- they can save up to £4,000 each year until age 50; and
- the government will make an additional 25 per cent contribution to the savings in the account.

The funds in this new ISA must either:

- be used to assist with the purchase of a first home costing up to £450,000; or
- withdrawn tax-free after an individual reaches age 60.

Failing this, the government bonus, plus any interest or growth in the account, must be repaid. A 5 per cent levy will also be charged.

Monies saved through a Lifetime ISA count towards the annual ISA subscription limit.

## Help-to-Save

Launched in September 2018, the Help-to-Save Scheme, a government-backed secure savings account, is:

- targeted at those on low incomes; and
- to help them boost their savings.

You can open a Help-to-Save account if you are either:

- entitled to Working Tax Credit; or
- claiming Universal Credit.

The benefits of a Help-to-Save Scheme include the following:

- You can contribute up to £50 each calendar month over four years.
- You do not have to save every month.
- You get a tax-free bonus of 50p for every £1 you save. Bonuses are paid at the end of the second and fourth years based on the amount of your savings.
- You close your account whenever you want. But you may miss the next bonus and you cannot open another account.

After four years your account will be closed, and you can retain all the funds in it.

The government has confirmed the scheme, initially intended to end in April 2025, will be extended until 5 April 2027.

# Enterprise Investment Scheme

The aims of the scheme are twofold:

- To provide a targeted incentive for equity investment in unquoted trading companies, which helps overcome the problems faced by such companies in raising modest amounts of equity finance.
- To encourage outside investors previously unconnected with the company, who introduce finance and expertise, by allowing them actively to participate in the management of the company as paid directors without losing entitlement to relief.

There are several features of EIS.

- Income Tax relief at 30 per cent on qualifying investments up to £1 million in a tax year. The limit is £2 million if at least £1 million of that sum is invested in knowledge-intensive companies.
- Subject to the annual £1 million subscription limit, the Income Tax relief can be carried back to the previous year.
- All shares in a qualifying company must be held for at least three years, otherwise the Income Tax relief will be clawed back.
- Losses made on the disposal of qualifying shares are eligible for relief from either Income Tax or Capital Gains Tax.

# Seed Enterprise Investment Scheme

This scheme runs alongside the EIS; but is targeted at smaller companies in the early stage of their development.

There are several features of SEIS.

- Income Tax relief at 50 per cent on qualifying investments up to £200,000 in a tax year.
- The 50 per cent rate of relief does not depend on the investor's top personal tax rate; it is calculated on the amount invested and given as a credit against the investor's total tax liability.

- The Income Tax relief can be carried back to the previous year.
- All shares in a qualifying company must be held for at least three years, otherwise the Income Tax relief will be clawed back.

## Venture Capital Trusts

Venture Capital Trusts (VCTs) are a type of Investment Trust with tax advantages designed to encourage investment in the under-nourished small business sector. Individuals investing in VCTs are eligible for the following Income Tax incentives.

- Relief at 30 per cent on subscriptions for new ordinary shares up to £200,000 in any tax year, providing the shares are held for at least five years.
- Tax-free dividends.

The 30 per cent Income Tax relief is deductible from the total Income Tax payable and does not depend on the investing individual's marginal tax rate.

## Overseas investment income

Generally, income from investments or savings abroad is taxed in the same way as your onshore dividends or interest income. Foreign tax paid, subject to certain restrictions, can be offset against the tax payable here on the same income. If required, you must be able to show that you have actually paid, or suffered, the overseas tax.

## Joint income

Income from assets such as bank/building society accounts, property or shares held in the joint names of a married couple or civil partners is treated for tax purposes as belonging to them in equal proportions. If the actual proportions of ownership between the couple are unequal, they can make an election for the income on any jointly owned assets to be taxed in accordance with their respective entitlements to the income, for example through a declaration of trust. There is a special form, Form 17, to complete. The declaration applies from the date it is made.

But dividends from jointly owned shares in a small family company are taxed on each spouse or civil partner according to their actual ownership, rather than in equal shares.

> **Tax Saver**
>
> Income splitting is likely to be of relevance to some taxpayers as a means of reducing their overall tax burden in view of:
>
> - the restriction to the personal allowance for individuals with incomes of more than £100,000; and
> - the 45 per cent rate of Income Tax on incomes in excess of £125,140.

# 11
# The family unit

Gone are the days when nearly all couples married. Many now prefer to live together as partners. Couples may have children without marrying, or marry later on in life.

## Living together

There are no special tax breaks for couples living with one another as partners. They are each taxed as single people. Furthermore, it is mandatory that income from jointly owned assets must be split between them in accordance with the ratio of their respective interests in such assets. Assets cannot be transferred between them without avoiding a possible liability to Capital Gains Tax at the time of transfer.

## Marriage/civil partnership

Spouses or civil partners are taxed separately on their income and capital gains. The following also applies.

- Each is entitled to personal allowances that can be set against their own income, whether from earnings or investments.
- They can each have taxable income, after allowances and reliefs, of £37,000 for 2024/25 before either of them is liable to tax at the higher rate of 40 per cent (they may, of course, need to rearrange their affairs to take maximum advantage of potential tax savings; in contrast to the position of unmarried couples this is easily done).
- Partners must complete their own Tax Returns every year, if required.
- They are each responsible for settling their respective tax liabilities.
- Note that the income limit for a married couple's allowance will rise to £37,700 in 2025/26.

# Children

A child or teenager is:

- treated as an individual for tax purposes like anyone else;
- entitled to the personal allowance – £12,570 for 2024/25 – so no tax is payable on any earnings or other income up to this limit; and
- a taxable person for the purposes of Capital Gains Tax (Chapter 13) and Inheritance Tax (Chapter 17).

But, the income from a gift by a parent in favour of an unmarried minor child is regarded as the parents' income for tax purposes – subject to an annual £100 limit for small amounts of income. The same restriction applies where the grandparent leaves money to their children in the Will but this is subsequently redirected to the grandchildren under a deed of variation for Inheritance Tax planning reasons.

> **Tax Saver**
>
> Relatives other than parents can, however:
>
> - give savings to their grandchildren, nieces, nephews, etc, without the same restrictions applying to the taxation of income on any such gifts; or
> - with the benefit of professional advice, set up a discretionary settlement with grandchildren among the class of beneficiaries. Such trusts suffer tax at 45 per cent on their income. As a result, taking the personal allowance into account, all or some of the tax suffered by the trustees on the income paid out for the benefit of a minor beneficiary should be repayable.

> A few years ago Jeremy Chandler created a discretionary trust. In 2024/25 the trustees resolved to distribute income of £2,000 for the benefit of his young granddaughter, Veronica. This is her only income in the year. Her parents can recover Income Tax of £1,636 for Veronica as follows:
>
> |  | Income (£) | Tax (£) |
> | --- | --- | --- |
> | Trust distribution | 3,636 | 1,636 |
> | *Less*: Personal allowance | 12,570 |  |
> | Taxable income | Nil |  |
> | Repayment for 2024/25 |  | 1,636 |

Parents, civil partners or those responsible for children do not get a general tax allowance for their children. However, there are other ways to claim benefits of tax credits if you are responsible for children.

- You should be able to claim Child Benefit. It does not depend on income.
- If you are on a low or modest income, you should be able to claim Universal Credit. Existing claimants may be receiving Child Tax Credit.
- Depending on your personal circumstances you may be entitled to one or more of the numerous other Social Security benefits associated with children.

It is down to parents or guardians to complete and sign Tax Returns or Repayment Claims for their children up to age 18.

# High Income Child Benefit Charge

This is a charge on a taxpayer:

- who has net income of more than £60,000 in a tax year; and
- either they, or their partner, is receiving Child Benefit.

Where both spouses or partners have net incomes exceeding £60,000, the charge is paid by the spouse or partner with the higher income.

The tax liability:

- is charged at 1 per cent for each £200 of net income between £60,000 and £80,000; and
- is equal to the amount of Child Benefit where net income exceeds £60,000.

Claimants of Child Benefit can opt not to receive the benefit if they or their spouse/partner want to avoid paying the charge.

---

In 2024/25, Joel Haynes' income is £70,000. They receive Child Benefit of £2,212.60, meaning their High Income Child Benefit Charge will be £1,106 (or 50 per cent of the £2,212.60).

## Tax-Free Childcare

This scheme is available for working families, whether:

- employed;
- self-employed; or
- on parental, sick or annual leave,

to help with the cost of childcare.
  To qualify, parents:

- must be in work; and
- earn at least the National Minimum Wage or Living Wage for working 16 hours a week. This works out at £183 for anyone aged 23 or over; but
- not more than £100,000 a year.

For every 80p contributed by eligible families the government will put in 20p, thereby providing support of up to £2,000 a year for each child. This limit doubles for a child with a disability.
  The scheme is available for children under:

- the age of 12; or
- the age of 18 for those with disabilities.

Adopted children are eligible but foster children are not.
  The scheme operates through an online Childcare account with National Savings and Investments in conjunction with HMRC and replaces the Childcare Voucher Scheme.

## The Child Trust Fund

Child Trust Funds (CTFs) were available for children born between 1 September 2002 and 2 January 2011. The scheme closed in 2011 and was replaced with the Junior Individual Savings Account (Junior ISA).
  The main features of CTFs still in existence are:

- Up to £9,000 in total can be added to the fund each year by family and friends.
- All income and capital growth within a CTF is tax-free.
- It can be accessed at age 18.

There are a wide range of organizations offering CTF accounts linked to either cash deposits, unit trusts or even equities.

It is now possible for parents with CTFs to get a better deal by transferring the funds to JISAs.

# Junior Individual Savings Account

Any child resident in the United Kingdom, under the age of 18, and who does not have a CTF account, is eligible for a JISA.

## Tax Saver

- A JISA is a tax-efficient way to save for your child's future. There are several key features of a JISA savers should be aware of.
- The account can be opened and managed by the person with parental responsibility for the child.
- Up to a fixed amount can be invested each year.
- The annual investment limit for 2024/25 is £9,000.
- All returns are tax-free.
- Family or friends can also contribute up to the amount of the annual allowance.
- The funds in a JISA can be invested in cash or stocks and shares.
- It can be accessed by the child at age 18.

# Separation and divorce

A married couple are no longer considered to be living together when:

- they are separated by a Deed or Court Order; or
- they are living apart in such a way that permanent separation is inevitable.

If a married couple are entitled to the married couple's allowance, the full allowance can be claimed by the husband or wife for the tax year in which the marriage fails. However, if he or she remarries in the same year he or she cannot also claim that part of the allowance due for the period following the wedding.

Maintenance payments are tax-free in the hands of the recipient, but only limited tax relief is available to the payer of maintenance under a Court Order, Child Support Agency assessment or written agreement as follows.

- Either the payer or recipient must be born before 6 April 1935.
- The payment must be to the divorced or separated spouse.
- The maximum amount of tax relief to which the payer is entitled in 2024/25 is 10 per cent of the lesser of £4,280 or the actual maintenance paid each year.
- No tax relief can be claimed on maintenance paid to, or for the benefit of, children of the marriage.

The tax implications for civil partners who separate are no different to those for a married couple. Similarly the dissolution of a civil partnership has the same consequences as a divorce.

# Old age

When it comes to tax, getting older does not mean an easier life. Pensioners have to deal with the tax system in the same way as everyone else. Nevertheless, there are some factors that are only relevant to:

- the finances of elderly persons; and
- working out how much tax they must pay each year.

First and foremost comes the married couple's allowance. In Chapter 2 I explained how an older taxpayer calculates the amount of this allowance to which he or she is entitled. Of particular significance are the rules allowing elderly couples to transfer the married couple's allowance between them, which can sometimes save on tax.

In addition is the income limit for the married couple's allowance, which is by reference to the husband's income or that of the spouse/civil partner with a higher income as the case may be. These rules apply even if entitlement to this allowance arises because of the age of the other spouse/civil partner.

**The family unit**

On reaching State Pension retirement age (see Chapter 9) you have three options:

- retire and claim the State Pension;
- carry on working and claim the State Pension; or
- put off claiming the State Pension.

All pensions, including a State Pension, are taxable. There is, however, no mechanism to deduct any Income Tax at source from payment of the State Pension. Therefore, in addition to including a pensioner's personal allowance in the coding notice of an occupational or personal pension taxed under PAYE, a deduction from allowances equivalent to the annual amount of the State Pension is also incorporated.

If a pensioner's State Pension and other deductions exceeds his or her personal allowance, HMRC issue a 'K' Coding. The amount of the negative allowance is then added to the pension on which tax is paid.

Taxpayers approaching State Pension age should make sure that their Notice of Coding is changed to include an estimate of the amount of their State Pension for the year. Usually HMRC sends such taxpayers a Form P161 asking for details about pension entitlement. This information is then used to amend tax codes as appropriate.

Nowadays many people carry on working after they retire from their main job or self-employment. They may decide to make use of all the knowledge and experience built up during their working lives by setting up in business as a consultant, or take a part-time position in, for example, a retail outlet.

---

Owen Wilcox is single and age 69. During 2024/25 he received a State Pension of £156.20 per week and an annual pension from his previous employer of £8,000. To keep himself occupied he worked part time at his local DIY store, earning a weekly wage of £105 for 46 weeks of the year. Owen paid Income Tax for 2024/25 of £1,676.48 as follows:

|  | Income (£) | Less tax taken under PAYE (£) |
|---|---|---|
| State Pension | 8,122.40 | – |
| Occupational pension | 8,000 | 733.48 |

*(continued)*

*(Continued)*

|  | Income (£) | Less tax taken under PAYE (£) |
|---|---|---|
| Wages | 4,830 | 966 |
|  | 20,952.40 |  |
| *Less*: Personal allowance | 12,570 |  |
| Taxable income | 8,382.40 |  |
| Income Tax payable |  |  |
| £7,415 @ 20 per cent |  | 1,676.48 |

The tax code used for working out the Income Tax to be deducted from Owen's occupational pension is 542L. This is based on the difference between Owen's personal allowance of £12,570 and his State Pension of £8,382.40. Tax at the basic rate of 20 per cent, under a BR Cde, would have been deducted from Owen's wage from the DIY store.

---

### Tax Saver

Elderly couples, in particular, need to pay great care and attention to their respective incomes. They should make sure that their investments and savings are arranged such that they:

- do not lose out on the married couple's allowance, only for taxpayers born before 6 April 1935; and
- take maximum advantage, if possible, of the generous annual amount that can be invested in ISAs.

They should also remain mindful of the annual income limit above which this allowance is restricted. As a result it may benefit couples to transfer capital between them.

# Death

Sadly, death comes to all of us and has tax consequences for married couples, which are as follows.

- The married couple's allowance is not restricted in the year of death of either spouse.
- Where the husband dies first, he is due his full personal allowance in the year of death. If he cannot use up the full married couple's allowance, because he has a low income, then the balance can be transferred to his widow.
- If the wife dies before her husband, she will be due her full personal allowance in the year of death.

Civil partners are treated no differently.

# 12
# Residence and domicile

As a general rule Income Tax is charged by the United Kingdom on:

- an individual's income arising in the United Kingdom irrespective of whether that person is resident here; and
- overseas income belonging to an individual resident in the United Kingdom.

Apart from some special cases, the amount of tax you pay each year depends on:

- whether you are resident in the United Kingdom; and
- in some circumstances on your domicile.

Not only are the two concepts of residence and domicile of fundamental importance in working out an individual's liability to UK taxation on income, but they are equally relevant for the purposes of both Capital Gains Tax and Inheritance Tax.

## Residence

There are statutory rules to determine whether an individual is, or is not, a resident in the UK. Under the statutory residence test, an individual is tax resident if either of the following are met, namely:

- automatic residence test; or
- the sufficient ties test which determines residence status based on a combination of days spent in, and various ties with, the UK.

# The automatic residence test

If you can answer 'yes' to any one of the following overseas tests you are automatically not resident in the UK for that tax year.

- Did you spend less than 16 days in the UK?*
- Were you in the UK for less than 46 days and have you been not resident in the UK for all of the previous three tax years?
- Were you in full-time employment abroad and spent less than
    - 91 days in the UK; and
    - fewer than 31 of those days working in the UK?**

However, you are automatically UK resident for a tax year if you:

- are not automatically non-resident; and
- can reply 'yes' to any of these UK tests.

The UK tests questions include the following.

- Did you spend 183 days or more in the UK?
- Did you work full-time in the UK?
- Did you have a UK home in which you resided for more than 30 days, with no home abroad?***

*This test does not apply if you die in the tax year. It is then replaced by other tests.
**A day at work in the UK means that you spend at least three hours working in the UK on that day.
***A home in the UK is any property which is available to you for at least 91 days in the tax year.

# Sufficient ties test

This is an alternative test if you do not meet either the automatic overseas or UK residence tests.

Then, the UK residence for a tax year of either:

- an individual leaving the UK to go abroad (a 'leaver'); or
- a person coming to the UK from overseas (an 'arriver'),

depends on:

- how many days they spend in the UK; and
- how many of the following five connecting factors that they satisfy.

These are as follows.

- Is your family UK resident?
- Do you have accommodation in the UK which is available to you?
- Have you spent at least 40 days working in the UK?
- Have you been in the UK for more than 90 days during either of the last two tax years?
- Have you spent more time in the UK than in any other country? ('leavers' only).

If you are a 'leaver' and have been UK resident in any one of the last three tax years, your residence status is determined by the following table.

| Days spent in the UK | Only resident if you satisfy |
|---|---|
| Less than 16 | Always non-resident |
| 16 to 45 | Four or more connecting factors |
| 46 to 90 | Three or more connecting factors |
| 91 to 120 | Two or more connecting factors |
| 121 to 182 | One or more connecting factors |
| 183 and more | Always resident |

If you are:

- an 'arriver'; and
- have not been UK resident in any one of the last three tax years,

your residence status is governed by the following table.

| Days spent in the UK | Only resident if you satisfy |
|---|---|
| Less than 16 | Always non-resident |
| 16 to 45 | Always non-resident |
| 46 to 90 | Four or more connecting factors |
| 91 to 120 | Three or more connecting factors |
| 121 to 182 | Two or more connecting factors |
| 183 and more | Always resident |

## Working abroad: expenses

Tax relief is allowed on the costs you incur on travel expenses in relation to your overseas employment. Nor will you be taxed on the following expenses borne by your employer.

- The cost of board and lodging outside the United Kingdom.
- Your travelling expenses, which also extends to unlimited return visits to the United Kingdom during longer assignments abroad.
- The travelling expenses of your spouse, civil partner or children to visit you overseas. No more than two return visits by the same person are allowed each year and you must be working abroad for a continuous period of at least 60 days.

## Leaving the United Kingdom permanently

Where you go abroad to live permanently, or are outside the United Kingdom for three years or more, you will cease to be UK resident from the day following your departure.

Before you leave, ask your tax office for the special form (P85) relevant to individuals going abroad. You can use this form to claim tax relief or a tax refund for the year during which you leave the UK if you:

- worked or lived here;
- are leaving;
- may not come back; or
- are going to work abroad full time for at least one full tax year.

The information on the form will also enable HMRC to consider your residence position.

As a non-resident, you will not usually pay UK tax on:

- the State Pension; and
- interest on government securities.

## Allowances for non-UK residents

If you are not resident here but have taxable income in the United Kingdom, you may be able to reduce your tax bill by claiming UK tax allowances.

These will generally be the same as those granted to an individual resident in the United Kingdom and can be claimed by the following individuals:

- a national of a state within the European Economic Area;
- a present or former employee of the British Crown;
- a resident of the Isle of Man or the Channel Islands;
- a widow or widower of a Crown Servant;
- a person employed by a missionary society; or
- a person abroad for health reasons following UK residence.

> **Tax Saver**
>
> To claim the allowances to which you are entitled and any resulting tax repayment, you will need to complete form R43 available from HMRC.

Other non-resident individuals may be able to claim UK tax allowances under the Double Taxation Agreement concluded between the country where they are resident and the United Kingdom.

# Income from UK property

Many individuals rent out their homes while they are living or working overseas. You can apply to HMRC for a certificate authorizing your tenant, or managing agent, to make payments of rent to you without withholding any UK tax. If you do not apply for a certificate or one is not issued to you, tax at the basic rate must be withheld from all remittances of rent to you by your managing agent or tenant.

Whether or not tax is deducted by your tenant or letting agent, while you are non-UK resident you are still liable to UK tax on income arising from the letting out of your property here.

However, you will not have to pay any UK tax if your income from property after allowable expenses, and any other taxable income, is less than any UK tax allowances that you may be entitled to claim.

> **Tax Saver**
>
> Non-resident married couples or civil partners with let property in the United Kingdom should consider putting their properties into joint ownership. It might then be possible for both parties to claim their personal allowance in working out the tax payable on their respective shares of the rental income.

## Double taxation relief

If you move to a country with which the United Kingdom has concluded a Double Taxation Agreement, you may be able to claim partial or full exemption from UK tax on certain types of income. These can include pensions, annuities and dividends.

Furthermore, many Double Taxation Agreements contain clauses dealing with the special circumstances of:

- teachers and researchers;
- students and apprentices; and
- entertainers and sports people.

## Going abroad: Capital Gains Tax

You will remain within the charge to Capital Gains Tax if you have been resident in the United Kingdom for at least four out of the last seven years and within five complete years you return to take up residence for tax purposes again.

It follows that:

- gains realized in the tax year of departure will be taxed in that year; and
- all gains in subsequent years, including the year of return, will be subject to tax in the year when residence resumes.

However, profits made on assets bought and sold during the years of non-UK tax residence are tax-free in the United Kingdom.

> Albert Rogers, who had lived his whole life in the United Kingdom, accepted an offer to work abroad and left the United Kingdom on 27 March 2019. On 17 July 2019 he sold an investment, which he owned when he left the United Kingdom, realizing a profit of £25,000. He returned to the United Kingdom to take up residence again on 3 November 2020.
>
> As Albert:
>
> - had only been abroad for three complete tax years (2019/20, 2020/21 and 2021/22); and
> - was a resident in the United Kingdom for at least four of the seven tax years preceding his departure,
>
> he will have to pay Capital Gains Tax on the gain of £25,000 in 2024/25.

# Residential property in the United Kingdom

If you are non-resident or resident, and have sold or disposed of UK residential property, you must tell HMRC within 60 days of conveyance.

You have to report the disposal within this time limit even if:

- the disposal results in a loss;
- there is no tax to pay; or
- you are already registered for Self Assessment.

The sale for CGT purposes takes place at exchange of contract, but the requirement to report and pay any tax is within 60 days of completion, rather than exchange. Taxpayers must also include the disposable gain on their Self Assessment where relevant.

Only that part of the gain relating to the period after 5 April 2015 is taxable. There are two ways of working this out. Either by:

- establishing the value of the property on 5 April 2015 and then calculating the gain based on this amount; or
- apportioning the gain equally over the total period of ownership.

The following chapter on capital gains sets out:

- the various reliefs; and
- the rates of tax,

for working out how much tax will be payable on the profit you made.

## Coming to the United Kingdom permanently

Perhaps you have been working overseas, your contract has finished and you have decided to return home; or you lived abroad and have now accepted a job offer in the United Kingdom.

You should:

- let HMRC know when you arrive in the United Kingdom; and
- apply for a NINO if you do not already have one and intend to work here.

You can claim the full UK personal allowance for the year of arrival. Where your job is with either a UK or an overseas employer and the duties of that employment will be performed wholly in the United Kingdom, the full amount of your salary will be taxable here.

> ### Tax Saver
>
> Before you leave the country where you have been living there may be opportunities to save on UK tax before taking up residence here. For example, it may pay you to close any bank or building society accounts before arrival as you would otherwise face the prospect of a charge to UK Income Tax on interest accrued, but not credited, while abroad.

## Domicile

Domicile:

- is a concept of general law; and
- is distinct from residence or nationality.

When you are born you acquire a domicile of origin from your father. Until you are 16 years old your domicile follows that of the person on whom you are legally dependent. At age 16 you have the option to abandon your existing domicile in favour of a domicile of choice. To do so you must sever all links and leave your current country or state and settle elsewhere. You will need to provide good evidence of your intention to live there indefinitely or permanently.

A wife's domicile is not necessarily the same as her husband's if they were married after the end of 1973. It is governed by the same factors as for any other individual with an independent domicile. However, a woman who married before the beginning of 1974 automatically acquired her husband's domicile on marriage. As long as the marriage lasts, her domicile only alters when there is any change in the domicile of her husband.

# Changes in tax treatment of non-domiciliaries

In the Autumn Statement 2024, the Chancellor announced the closure of several 'loopholes', with plans to legislate against the remittance basis of taxation for non-UK domiciled individuals, or 'non-doms'.

From 6 April 2025, this is being replaced by a new residence-based regime. Individuals who opt into the regime will not pay UK tax on foreign income and gains (FIG) for the first four years of their residency. Individuals can access this, provided they have not been a UK tax resident in any of the 10 consecutive years prior to their arrival.

Individuals ineligible for this new residence-based scheme will be subject to CGT on FIG in the normal way.

In announcing this, the government also made available a Temporary Repatriation Facility (TRF) for individuals who have been taxed on the remittance basis. Individuals that have previously claimed remittance basis will be able to remit FIG that arose prior to 6 April 2025, and pay a reduced tax rate on their remittance for a limited time period.

# 13
# Capital gains

The profits you make on disposing of your assets are known as capital gains and are subject to Capital Gains Tax. However, not all capital receipts are taxable. These include:

- lottery, pools or gambling winnings;
- mortgage cash-backs; and
- personal or professional damages.

Profits made on disposing of the following assets are also tax-free:

- private cars;
- National Savings;
- your home;
- chattels sold for less than £6,000;
- British government securities and many corporate bonds;
- shares issued under either the EIS or SEIS as long as the Income Tax relief has not been withdrawn;
- shares in VCTs;
- shares issued under an employee shareholder agreement;
- investments in an ISA;
- gifts to charities or for the public benefit; and
- qualifying life policies on your life.

## Taxable gains

This list includes profits you realize from disposing of:

- property;
- shares and unit trust investments; or
- chattels sold for more than £6,000.

For Capital Gains Tax purposes, the date when the contract for purchase or sale is made determines the date when an asset is acquired or sold.

# Tax payable

Every tax year you can make gains up to the annual exemption limit without paying tax. For 2024/25 the tax-free allowance is £3,000. Chargeable gains over and above this limit are taxed at different flat rates depending on both the type of asset sold and your income.

| Band of taxable income (£) | Residential property* (rate of tax %) | Other assets (rate of tax %) |
| --- | --- | --- |
| 0–37,700 | 18 | 18 |
| Above 37,700 | 28 | 24 |

*That which does not qualify for private residence relief; for example, buy-to-let.

These increased rates have only applied to disposals since the Autumn Budget in 2024.

> ### Tax Saver
>
> If, in the same tax year, you realize profits from selling both a buy-to-let and shares you can set your tax-free allowance against the gains taxed at the highest rate.

> In 2024/25 Alastair McLaren made gains of £27,000 and £8,000 from selling an investment property and shares respectively after 30 October. He pays tax at the higher rate. His Capital Gains Tax bill for the year is £8,640, as follows:
>
> |  | £ |
> | --- | --- |
> | Investment property gain | 27,000 |
> | Less: tax-free allowance | 3,000 |
> |  | 24,000 |
>
> *(continued)*

*(Continued)*

|  | £ |
|---|---|
| Profit on selling shares | 8,000 |
|  | 32,000 |
| Tax payable |  |
| £24,000 @ 28 per cent | 6,720 |
| 8,000 @ 24 per cent | 1,920 |
|  | 8,640 |

### Tax Saver

Wherever possible try to utilize your full Capital Gains Tax Allowance limit each year. Any unused part of the annual limit is lost. It cannot be carried forward to future years.

### Tax Saver

By realizing gains just after the end of a tax year you will delay payment of the tax for 12 months.

### Tax Saver

By splitting sales across the end of a tax year you can make use of your annual tax-free allowance for two years.

## Married couples/civil partners

Each spouse/civil partner is:

- separately entitled to the annual tax-free allowance limit; and
- individually taxed on chargeable gains they realize in a tax year in excess of the annual exemption limit.

A married couple living together can transfer assets between them without gain or loss as follows.

- The recipient spouse is deemed to have acquired such assets at the cost to the former spouse.
- This tax-free allowance ceases when a couple permanently separate.

It is not uncommon for a married couple to own assets in their joint names. For tax purposes, a profit on disposal of a jointly owned asset is apportioned between each spouse/civil partner in the ratio of their respective interests in that asset at the date of disposal.

> **Tax Saver**
>
> A husband and wife, or a couple in a civil partnership, each have their own annual exemption limit. They should consider transferring assets between them in order to use up both exemption limits.

> **Tax Saver**
>
> But this does not apply to married couples or civil partners who separate. The opportunity to transfer assets between them free of Capital Gains Tax terminates at least two years after the separation. The moral here is to separate early on in a tax year to allow sufficient time to divide up valuable assets such as land and shares. The 2003 Finance Act introduced new timelines Separating spouses or civil partners be given up to three years after the year they cease to live together in which to make no gain/no loss transfers. No gain/no loss treatment will also apply to assets that separating spouses or civil partners transfer between themselves as part of a formal divorce agreement.

# Working out chargeable gains

In calculating the taxable gain on the disposal of a chargeable asset, you are allowed to make certain deductions from the proceeds of sale as follows:

- the purchase price;

- incidental costs incurred on acquiring the asset;
- any additional expenditure you have incurred on enhancing the value of the asset; and
- the costs of sale.

The list of incidental expenses that are allowed as either purchase or sale costs includes:

- solicitor's fees, including transfer and conveyancing costs;
- surveyor's, valuer's or auctioneer's fees;
- broker's commission;
- estate agent's commission, including advertising expenses;
- Stamp Duty Land Tax; and
- valuation costs.

## Relief for losses

Losses and gains made in the same tax year are offset against each other. Any excess losses can be carried forward, without time limit, to reduce gains in subsequent tax years. But losses can never reduce the amount of your gains to below the annual exemption limit.

---

Bernard Levy had unused capital losses of £9,700 at 5 April 2024. During 2024/25 he made gains of £20,700 and incurred losses of £8,500. His capital gains position for the year is:

|  | £ | £ |
| --- | --- | --- |
| Gains realized in the year |  | 20,700 |
| *Less*: Losses |  |  |
| in the year | 8,500 |  |
| brought forward (part) | 6,200 |  |
|  |  | 6,000 |
| 2024/25 Exemption limit |  | 3,000 |

The unused losses at 5 April 2024 of £3,500 (£9,700 – £6,200) can be carried forward to be set against gains in later years.

A loss arising on the sale or gift of an asset to a person with whom you are connected can only be set off against a gain on a similar disposal at a later date.

A loss can also be claimed where the value of an asset you own becomes negligible or nil. You do not actually have to dispose of the asset. The loss arises on the date that the relief is claimed. In practice, however, a two-year period is allowed from the end of the tax year in which the asset became of negligible value. In some cases the loss can be offset against income, giving you a bigger tax refund.

## Business Asset Disposal Relief

Business Asset Disposal Relief (BADR) is a relief that can be claimed by individuals in working out their capital gains on the disposal of:

- all or part of a trading business carried on alone or in partnership;
- assets owned by an individual and used in his or her business;
- shares in an individual's own trading company; and
- shares in a trading company where an individual is an employee or officer of the company and:
  - owns at least 5 per cent of the company; or
  - has 5 per cent or more of the voting rights; and
  - from 29 October 2018 is entitled to at least 5 per cent of the distributable profits and net assets of the company.

The business, assets or shares, as the case may be, must be owned by the individual for at least two years prior to the date of disposal. However, on cessation a three-year time limit is allowed in which to make the disposal providing the individual satisfied the one-year requirement up to cessation.

From 6 April 2025, under BADR the rate of Capital Gains Tax payable is 14% on qualifying lifetime gains up to £1 million. This will rise from 6 April 2026 to match the lower rate of 18%.

Gains made on disposals before 6 April 2008 do not count towards the lifetime allowance.

> **Tax Saver**
>
> It may pay to look into how the ownership of your business is structured so that not only you, but also other family members, may be entitled to BADR in working out the Capital Gains Tax payable on the profit on a future sale or disposal of the business.

---

In November 2024 Martin Osborne sold the shares he owned in his own trading company for £460,000. He originally bought the company in 1995 for £190,000. This was his only disposal in 2024/25. Martin pays Capital Gains Tax for the year of £48,060 as follows:

|  | £ |
|---|---:|
| Proceeds of sale | 460,000 |
| *Less*: Purchase price | 190,000 |
| Gain qualifying for Business Asset Disposal Relief | 270,000 |
| *Less*: Annual exemption limit | 3,000 |
| Gain chargeable to tax | 267,000 |
| 2024/25 Capital Gains Tax @ 18 per cent | 48,060 |

# Investors' Relief

This is a relief on the disposal by investors of new ordinary shares in un-listed trading companies:

- subscribed for and fully paid in cash; and
- held for at least three years, starting from 6 April 2016.

There is no requirement for an investor to:

- be an officer or employee of the company; or
- hold more than 5 per cent of the shares or voting rights in it.

Like BADR, from 6 April 2025, under Investors' Relief the rate of Capital Gains Tax payable is 14 per cent on qualifying lifetime gains up to £1 million. This will rise from 6 April 2026 to match the lower rate of 18 per cent.

## Assets owned on 31 March 1982

Gains and losses on disposals of assets that you held on 31 March 1982 must be calculated solely by reference to their market value at that date, ignoring original costs.

> Ashley Barker acquired a freehold factory in the late 1970s for £25,000. It was valued at £30,000 on 31 March 1982. Ashley sold the factory in May 2024 for £120,000, after expenses of sale.
> The chargeable gain is £90,000 as follows:
>
> |  | £ |
> | --- | --- |
> | Sale price | 120,000 |
> | *Less*: March 1982 value | 30,000 |
> | 2024/25 chargeable gain | 90,000 |

## Investments in shares

When you buy shares, you usually pay a tax or duty of 0.50 per cent on the transaction. If you buy shares electronically, you'll pay Stamp Duty Reserve Tax (SDRT) whereas if you buy these via a stock transfer form you'll pay Stamp Duty if the transaction is over £1,000.

An important thing to remember is you will pay tax on the price you pay for the shares, even if their market value is much higher.

However, you do not have to pay tax if you:

- are given the shares for nothing;
- subscribe to a new issue of shares in a company;
- buy shares in an open-ended investment company (OEIC) for a fund manager; or
- buy units in a trust from a fund manager.

Most importantly, you will need to pay Capital Gains Tax when you sell your shares.

Where a company in which you have a holding is taken over and you receive shares in the new company in exchange for your shares in the company taken over, no disposal for tax purposes takes place at that time. Your new holding is regarded as having been acquired at the same time, and for the same price, as the old one. If, however, you receive a mixture of cash and shares in the new company, a gain or a loss arises on the cash element of the takeover. It is then necessary to apportion the cost price of the old shares between the cash received and the value of the shareholding in the new company at the time.

# Your home

The profit on the sale of your home is free of tax. The exemption automatically covers the house, and the gardens or grounds up to half a hectare (including the land on which the house is built).

A larger area of land can qualify for exemption where it can be shown that it was required for reasonable enjoyment of the house.

For the exemption to apply in full you must live in your house throughout:

- the full period of ownership; or
- if later, since 31 March 1982.

If you build your own house, the period of ownership only applies when you start to occupy the home.

Where your home fails to meet all the exemption requirements, a proportion of the gain on sale is taxable.

## Tax Saver

Certain periods of absence are, however, disregarded in determining whether the gain is totally tax-free.

These are:

- the last nine months of ownership always; and
- generally when you have to live away from home because of your work.

But this period extends to one of 36 months if:

- you are disabled; or
- move into long-term residential care.

However, while this allows the property to qualify as a residence it does not necessarily make this a main residence for CGT exemption. Please consult with the HMRC for further details if unsure.

---

Guy Robinson sold his home in February 2024, making a profit of £90,000 as worked out for Capital Gains Tax purposes. He had bought the property in November 2015.

His job had taken him abroad between March 2017 and May 2019. Shortly after his return he bought a new home and moved there in August 2018.

The time spent working abroad and the last nine months from August 2021 are also considered periods when the property was Guy's main residence. Provided he sent a suitable nomination to HMRC, the chargeable gain is, therefore, restricted to the part of the gain apportioned to the two years between August 2019 and August 2021 as follows:

$$\frac{\text{Chargeable period}}{\text{Period of ownership}} = \frac{24 \text{ months}}{87 \text{ months}} \times £90{,}000 = £24{,}827$$

---

### Tax Saver

It is usually possible to make sure that the whole house has some non-business use, such as using the office for personal use or by the family at weekends.

## Stamp Duty Land Tax

You must pay Stamp Duty Land Tax (SDLT) if you buy property or land over a certain price in England and Northern Ireland – differences apply in Scotland and Wales.

As with many taxes, thresholds apply with SDLT. From 1 April 2025 these are as follows:

- £125,000 for residential properties;
- £300,000 for first-time buyers of residential properties worth £500,000 or less;
- £150,000 for non-residential land or properties.

And, also as with many other taxes, the rates of SDLT vary and this can also depend on the kind of arrangement such as when property is being purchased by a trust or corporate body. For the sake of simplicity, here are the residential SDLT rates from 1 April 2025:

0 to 125,000: 0%
125,001 to 250,000: 2%
250,001 to 925,000: 5%
925,001 to 1,500,000: 10%
1,500,001 and above: 12%

# A second home

It is not uncommon these days for individuals to have two properties. The main home is usually a house or flat within a commutable distance from the office or other place of work. The second property might be in the country, by the seaside or abroad in a warmer climate.

If you are buying an additional property, and this will not be replacing your main residence, there is an additional rate of SDLT to pay on this.

From 31 October 2024, the rates of SDLT on second homes were changed. These were increased from 3 per cent to 5 per cent.

> **Tax Saver**
>
> It is only the profit on the sale of your main residence that is free of tax. Which one of your two or more homes is considered your main residence is usually a matter of fact. There is a two-year time limit for such nominations from the moment of the second home purchase. It is, however, possible for you to determine this in writing to your tax office. In the election, you should state which of your homes you want regarded as your principal private

residence for Capital Gains Tax purposes. Both homes must be your home, meaning you cannot rent out either property.

But you can only nominate an overseas property if you lived in it for at least 90 days in the tax year.

### Tax Saver

Spouses/civil partners are only allowed one qualifying home between them.

However, spouses/civil partners should certainly consider owning a second home jointly. This could help reduce the Capital Gains Tax payable on a future sale as they may both be able to take advantage of their respective annual exemption limits in working out the tax payable on a profit on sale.

It is not uncommon for unmarried couples or civil partners to each own a home. They may each be able to nominate a main residence for the purposes of Capital Gains Tax.

If you own a home that was occupied rent-free by a dependent relative, then the profit on sale attributable to both their periods of occupation:

- up to 5 April 1988; and
- thereafter,

is tax-free.

## Chattels

Profits from selling chattels with an expected life of more than 50 years that are sold for less than £6,000 are tax-free. Chattels include paintings and other works of art, antiques, furniture, jewellery, stamps and ornaments. Articles comprising a set are considered as a single item when they are sold to the same person but at different times.

For items that fetch between £6,000 and £15,000, the chargeable gain is restricted to 5/3 times the amount by which the proceeds of sale (ignoring expenses) exceeds £6,000 where this is to your advantage.

When an article is sold for under £6,000 and at a loss, the allowable loss is restricted by assuming the sale proceeds were equal to £6,000.

> Vincent Wells bought a set of stamps in the late 1980s for £8,300. The set was sold in December 2024 for £6,600. Vincent's allowable loss is £1,700. If he had only made £3,800 on the sale, the tax loss would have been £2,300 (£8,300 – £6,000).

# Gifts and valuations

There are times when a figure different from the actual disposal proceeds is used in the calculation of a capital gain. This happens, for example, when you make a gift or sell an asset at a nominal value to a close member of your family. On these occasions, you must work out the capital gain based on the open-market value of the asset at the time of gift or disposal.

There is a free service from HMRC that will help you whenever you need to use valuations to work out a gain or loss.

After you have made a disposal but before you make your return:

- you need to ask for one copy of Form CG34 for each valuation you want checked and confirmed; and
- you must then return the completed form to your tax office at least two months before the filing date for the Tax Return together with all the other information and documents requested on the form.

Agreed valuations will not subsequently be challenged when you submit your Tax Return unless you did not previously mention important facts affecting the valuations. If your figures are not agreed, HMRC will put forward alternative valuations.

> **Tax Saver**
>
> Where the gift is one of a qualifying business asset, you can elect jointly with the transferee for payment of the tax on the gift to be postponed until the asset is subsequently disposed of by the transferee.

# Short life assets

Short life, or wasting, assets are those with an expected lifespan of less than 50 years. A gain on the disposal of a wasting asset is worked out in the same way as that on the disposal of any other asset, except that the purchase price wastes away during the expected lifespan of the asset.

Leases of land for less than 50 years are wasting assets. There is a specific formula for calculating the proportion of the purchase price of a lease that can be deducted from the sale proceeds.

The gain or loss on the sale of a wasting asset that is also 'tangible moveable property' is outside of tax.

## Part disposals

There are several points to be aware of when you dispose of only part of an asset you own.

- You apportion the acquisition cost between the part sold and the fraction retained. This is worked out on a pro-rata basis by reference to the sale proceeds of the part sold and the open-market value of the proportion retained.
- The proportion of the cost price of the asset attributable to the part retained can be set against the proceeds on the sale of the remainder at a later date.
- If the part sold is small compared with the value of the whole asset, you can simply deduct the sale proceeds from the acquisition cost. Where the part disposal is one of land, this procedure can be followed so long as the sale proceeds are less than both £20,000 and one-fifth of the value of the remaining land.

## Enterprise Investment Scheme

A profit on disposing of qualifying shares under the EIS is free of Capital Gains Tax, provided:

- the Income Tax relief originally allowed on the investment has not been withdrawn; and
- the disposal takes place at least three years after the issue of the shares.

If you incur a loss on disposing of qualifying shares you can offset the loss, after taking off any Income Tax relief allowed, against either:

- capital gains in the same year that the loss is realized; or

- your taxable income in the year of loss, or the previous year.

It is also possible to defer Capital Gains Tax payable on chargeable gains by reinvesting the gains in qualifying EIS shares. For deferral relief purposes the chargeable gains must be reinvested in the period beginning one year before, and ending three years after, the original disposal. Deferral relief can be claimed:

- along with both Income Tax relief (see Chapter 10) and exemption from Capital Gains Tax (as above) up to an annual investment limit of £1 million;
- on its own as the amount of gains that can be deferred is unlimited; or
- in any other combination you choose within the rules.

If deferral relief is claimed, the original liability to Capital Gains Tax will crystallize when the EIS shares are sold.

# SEIS

A gain on disposing of shares qualifying under the SEIS is not chargeable to Capital Gains Tax provided:

- the Income Tax Relief granted on the investment has not been withdrawn; and
- the disposal does not occur within three years after the shares have been issued.

> **Tax Saver**
>
> You can claim exemption from Capital Gains Tax on half of your capital gains up to a maximum of £100,000 where the profit is re-invested in a SEIS. As a consequence, the maximum gains free of Capital Gains Tax are £50,000.

# VCTs

A profit on disposal of shares in a VCT is exempt from Capital Gains Tax provided:

- the original subscription for the shares disposed of did not exceed the maximum permitted investment limit in the year of purchase, £200,000 for 2024/25; and

- the company qualifies as a VCT both at the time the shares are acquired and at the date of disposal.

## Inheritances

No Capital Gains Tax is payable on the unrealized profits on your assets as at the date of your death. When you inherit an asset you acquire it at the value on the date of death of the deceased. Generally, this rule is also applied whenever you become entitled to assets from a Trust.

# 14

# How to complete your Tax Return and work out your tax

This tax guide is being published shortly after HMRC have sent out emails, letters or Tax Returns:

- requiring taxpayers, by law, to make a Return of their taxable income and capital gains for the year from 6 April 2023 to 5 April 2024; and
- to claim the allowances and tax reliefs to which they are entitled for the same year.

## Do I need to complete a Tax Return?

You probably don't need to complete a Tax Return if your tax affairs are not complicated; and you receive income taxed under PAYE.

But you may need to fill one in if your tax affairs are not straightforward, and you receive income from several sources.

## Who has to complete a Tax Return?

HMRC will want a Tax Return from you each year if you:

- earn more than £50,000 and either you, your wife or partner is receiving Child Benefit;
- are self-employed and earn more than £1,000;
- are a company director;

- have been issued with a notice to complete a self-assessment return;
- are a partner in a partnership;
- have a capital gains liability after allowing for the Capital Gains Tax annual exemption;
- own land or property in the United Kingdom from which you receive rental income;
- have other untaxed income and it is not possible to collect the tax due through your PAYE tax code;
- make capital gains in excess of the annual exemption limit; or
- are an employee or pensioner with more complex tax affairs.

## Employees and pensioners with complex tax affairs

You must fill in a Tax Return if you:

- have an annual salary or pension of at least £150,000 (but the £150,000 limit has been removed from 2024/25);
- receive income from savings or investments of at least £10,000 (before tax) in a year;
- hold shares on which the annual dividends are £10,000 or more (before tax) annually;
- have untaxed income in excess of £2,500; or
- owe tax at the end of the year that cannot be collected in the following year through your PAYE tax code.

## How do I register for Self Assessment?

HMRC is strongly recommending and encouraging taxpayers to file online because:

- it is secure and convenient;
- tax calculations are done for you automatically;
- on-screen help is available if you need it;

# How to complete your Tax Return and work out your tax

- you get an immediate acknowledgement that your Return has been received; and
- if you are owed money, you will get a faster repayment.

You can also:

- see whether HMRC owe you money, or how much you owe HMRC;
- view your statement of account for the last three years;
- make changes to your personal contact details; and
- make a claim to reduce payments on account or request a refund (if your account is in credit).

You need to visit www.gov.uk/register-for-self-assessment:

- if you are not already registered for Self Assessment; and
- to file your Tax Return online with HMRC's free online service.

You must register by 5 October 2025 if you have to file a Tax Return for 2024/25. Should you miss this deadline you may become liable to a penalty.
You will need:

- your NINO; and
- information about your business (if applicable).

At the end of the registration process, HMRC will give you a Unique Taxpayer Reference (UTR).
To file a Tax Return online you need an HMRC online account. If you are not given an account when you register you can sign up for one through HMRC's online services.

## Filing deadlines

The deadline for filing your 2024/25 Tax Return online is 31 January 2026. If you decide to complete a paper Tax Return for 2024/25 you must send it back by 31 October 2025 so HMRC has time:

- to work out the tax you owe or the refund due to you; and
- to let you know the result of their calculation before the 31 January 2026 payment deadline.

> **Tax Saver**
>
> Unless your preference is to make a direct payment by 31 January 2026, HMRC will, if possible, collect the tax you owe for the year through next year's tax code so long as they either:
>
> - receive your paper 2024/25 Tax Return by 31 October 2024; or
> - you file online by 30 December 2025
>
> and you:
>
> - owe tax of not more than £3,000; and
> - have a PAYE tax code.
>
> There is no interest or other charge for spreading out the tax under payment for 2024/25 over income received in 2026/27.

# The Tax Return

The Tax Return runs to eight pages. Also available from HMRC are:

- a Tax Return guide;
- supplementary colour-coded pages based on your tax history; and
- a separate four-page section of Additional Information pages for dealing with the less common types of income and tax reliefs.

The list of the various supplementary pages is as follows:

| | |
|---|---|
| Employment | Pink |
| Self-employment | Orange |
| Partnership | Turquoise |
| UK property | Red |
| Foreign | Mustard |
| Trusts etc | Brown |
| Capital gains summary | Blue |
| Residence, remittance basis, etc | Green |

# Getting started

Try to avoid the temptation of putting off the job of filling in your Return. It is better to get on with it as soon as you can because you will:

- have more time to get help from HMRC if you need it;
- have more time to save for any tax you owe; and
- get a big weight off your mind!

> **Tax Saver**
>
> Getting started as soon as possible is a must if you have paid too much tax. HMRC will refund any overpayment direct to your bank or building society. This is the safest and quickest method. Always fill in boxes 4–14 on page TR6 as appropriate.

Start by going to page TR2. This will help you decide which, if any, supplementary pages you need. These can be obtained by:

- telephoning the order line on 0300 200 3610 (open seven days a week from 8 am to 10 pm); or
- going to www.gov.uk/self-assessment-forms-and-helpsheets to download them.

The supplementary pages come with notes to help you fill in the pages you requested. Helpsheets, explanatory booklets and leaflets that may also further assist you in working out the income or capital gains to be declared are similarly available from HMRC, and listed in Appendix 6.

# Keeping proper records

> **Tax Saver**
>
> First and foremost, keep proper and orderly records as this will make it easier for you to complete your Tax Return fully and accurately.

> • In addition, if the tax office decides to enquire into your Tax Return you will be able to demonstrate that the Return is both accurate and complete from the records you have maintained.

Before you start filling in your Tax Return you need to gather together all the information on your income, capital gains, reliefs and allowances from the records you have been keeping for the year to 5 April 2025. For most types of income and capital gains you only need to retain the records given to you by whoever provided that income or realized the gains for you.

- If you are in employment you will need:
  - your Form P60, a certificate your employer will give you after 5 April (the end of the tax year) detailing your pay and the tax deducted from it;
  - Form P11D or P9D or equivalent information from your employer showing any benefits-in-kind and expenses payments you received;
  - any Form P45 (part 1A) certificate from an employer showing pay and tax from a job you have left;
  - any Form P160 (part 1A) you may have been given when you retire and then go on to receive a pension from your former employer;
  - your payslips or pay statements;
  - a note of the amount of any tips or gratuities along with details of any other taxable receipts.
- If you are receiving a UK pension or Social Security benefits you will need:
  - your Form P60, a certificate given to you by the payer of your occupational pension, stating the amount of your pension and the tax deducted;
  - a certificate detailing any other pension you received and the tax deducted from it;
  - information given to you by the DWP relating to state pensions, taxable state benefits, Statutory Sick, Maternity or Paternity Pay and the JSA.

## How to complete your Tax Return and work out your tax

- If you are letting out property you will need records of:
  - the dates when your property is rented;
  - all the rents you receive;
  - bills and invoices for all the allowable expenses you incur to run and manage your property.
- If receiving investment income, you'll need records of the following:
  - bank and building society statements, passbooks and tax deduction certificates;
  - statements of interest and any other income received from your savings and investments; for example, an annuity;
  - vouchers for dividends received from UK companies;
  - unit trust tax vouchers;
  - life insurance chargeable event certificates;
  - details of any income you received from a trust or the estate of a deceased person;
  - information about any exceptional amounts – such as an inheritance or other windfall – that you receive and subsequently invest.
- If you are making capital gains, or losses, you will need:
  - contracts for the purchase or sale of shares, unit trusts, property or any other assets;
  - copies of any valuations you need to work out your capital gains or losses;
  - bills, invoices or other evidence of payment records such as bank statements and cheque stubs for costs you claim for the purchase, improvement or sale of assets;
  - details of any assets you have given away or put into a trust.
- And when claiming personal allowances, other deductions or reliefs, you will need records of:
  - certificates of interest paid on any loans that qualify for tax relief;
  - declarations you have made to charities of gifts under Gift Aid;
  - receipts for the payment of pension premiums;
  - notification that you are registered as a blind person.

This list of the types of records you are advised to keep is not exhaustive and does not cover every situation. If you are in any doubt, ask your tax office for assistance.

Prudent taxpayers should keep their records for seven years in case there is an HMRC enquiry.

## Filling in your Tax Return

The paper Tax Return is designed to be read by a machine. It is important to complete the form properly so that it is correctly read.

> **Tax Saver**
>
> Always:
>
> - use black ink and capital letters;
> - cross out any mistakes and write the correct information below;
> - enter figures in whole pounds, ignoring pence;
> - round down income;
> - round up expenses and tax paid – this will benefit you;
> - write in the spaces provided; and
> - if a box does not apply simply leave it blank.

There is not enough space to reproduce the eight-page Tax Return, as well as the Additional Information and supplementary pages. In the following pages, you will find reproductions of the supplementary page on Employment, most of the sections for the Tax Return and some of those from the Additional Information pages. All of these have been sourced from HMRC.

If you have more than one job you will need to fill in a separate employment page for each job as follows.

- In Box 1 enter your before-tax salary or wage from your P60 or P45.
- Enter the tax taken off your pay in Box 2.
- Tips and other payments not on your P60 go in Box 3.

# How to complete your Tax Return and work out your tax

- The PAYE tax reference of your employer, which will be shown on your P60 or P45, needs to be entered in Box 4.
- Box 5 is for your employer's name.
- Use your Form P11D, or equivalent information, to enter the taxable amounts of any benefits from your employment in Boxes 9 to 16.
- Any business travel or subsistence expenses, professional fees and subscriptions and other expenses paid by you and on which you can claim tax relief go in Boxes 17 to 20.

Leaving aside the sections on the first two pages of the Tax Return asking for your personal details, the first part of page TR3 is for you to report your interest and dividend income as follows.

- You may have received interest where tax has been taken off at source. If so, enter the after-tax figure in Box 1.
- In Box 2 you should enter the total of the amounts of interest on all your UK bank, building society and other interest-bearing accounts where no tax has been deducted.
- If you have received any interest from overseas not exceeding £2,000, then this amount goes in Box 3.
- The total of all your dividends in the year should be entered in Box 4.
- You should do likewise in completing Box 5 in respect of any dividends received from authorized unit trusts and open-ended investment companies.
- Boxes 6 and 7 are for your foreign dividends, up to £300, and the tax taken off these foreign dividends.

The next section on page TR3 deals with UK pensions, annuities and other State benefits received as follows.

- The figure to put in Box 8 is the total of your weekly entitlements to the State Pension, not the amount you actually received, even if you were paid monthly or quarterly. If you are unsure about the amount, telephone the Pension Direct Service on 0345 606 0265 and ask for this figure for the year from 6 April 2023 to 5 April 2024. Do not include either the Christmas bonus or your winter fuel payment as these are not taxable.
- You will only need to complete Boxes 9 and 10 if you received a State Pension lump sum in the year.
- All your other pension income, and the tax taken off, needs to be shown in Boxes 11 and 12. In Box 19 on page 7 you should separately list the names of the payers of your pensions, the amounts paid and the tax deducted.

## Figure 14.1

# Employment

Tax year 6 April 2024 to 5 April 2025 (2024–25)

**Your name**: TOM SMITH

**Your Unique Taxpayer Reference (UTR)**: 4 3 2 9 6   5 5 4 3 4

For help filling in this form, go to www.gov.uk/taxreturnforms and read the notes and helpsheets.

### Complete an 'Employment' page for each employment or directorship

1. Pay from this employment – the total from your P45 or P60 – before tax was taken off: £ 37440.00

2. UK tax taken off pay in box 1: £ –8553.00

3. Tips and other payments not on your P60:

4. PAYE tax reference of your employer (on your P45/P60): 28 / B604

5. Your employer's name: BROADWOOD ENGINEERS LTD

6. If you were a company director, put 'X' in the box

6.1 If you ceased being a director before 6 April 2020, put the date the directorship ceased in the box DD MM YYYY

7. And, if the company was a close company, put 'X' in the box

8. If you're a part-time teacher in England or Wales and are on the Repayment of Teachers' Loans Scheme for this employment, put 'X' in the box

8.1 If box 1 includes any disguised remuneration income, put 'X' in the box – read the notes

### Benefits from your employment – use your form P11D (or equivalent information)

9. Company cars and vans: £ 4000.00

10. Fuel for company cars and vans: £ 4520.00

11. Private medical and dental insurance: £ 900.00

12. Vouchers, credit cards and excess mileage allowance:

13. Goods and other assets provided by your employer:

14. Accommodation provided by your employer:

15. Other benefits (including interest-free and low interest loans):

16. Expenses payments received and balancing charges:

### Employment expenses

17. Business travel and subsistence expenses:

18. Fixed deductions for expenses:

19. Professional fees and subscriptions:

20. Other expenses and capital allowances:

**SOURCE** HMRC

## Figure 14.2

Interest and dividends from UK banks, building societies etc

1 **Taxed UK interest etc** - the net amount after tax has been taken off - read the notes

£ 80 · 0 0

2 **Untaxed UK interest etc** - amounts which have not had tax taken off - read the notes

£ 240 · 0 0

3 **Untaxed foreign interest (up to £2,000)** - amounts which have not had tax taken off - read the notes

£ · 0 0

4 **Dividends from UK companies** - the amount received - read the notes

£ 1580 · 0 0

5 **Other dividends** - the amount received - read the notes

£ 190 · 0 0

6 **Foreign dividends (up to £300)** - the amount in sterling after foreign tax was taken off. Do not include this amount in the 'Foreign' pages

£ 160 · 0 0

7 **Tax taken off foreign dividends** - the sterling equivalent

£ 24 · 0 0

**SOURCE** HMRC

## Figure 14.3

UK pensions, annuities and other state benefits received

8 **State Pension** - amount you were entitled to receive in the year, **not the weekly or 4-weekly amount** - read the notes

£ 6550 · 0 0

9 **State Pension lump sum** - the gross amount of any lump sum - read the notes

£ · 0 0

10 **Tax taken off box 9**

£ · 0 0

11 **Pensions (other than State Pension), retirement annuities and taxable triviality payments** - the gross amount. Tax taken off goes in box 12

£ 21000 · 0 0

12 **Tax taken off box 11**

£ 3140 · 0 0

13 **Taxable Incapacity Benefit and contribution-based Employment and Support Allowance** - read the notes

£ · 0 0

14 **Tax taken off Incapacity Benefit in box 13**

£ · 0 0

15 **Jobseeker's Allowance**

£ · 0 0

16 **Total of any other taxable State Pensions and benefits**

£ · 0 0

**SOURCE** HMRC

- The remaining boxes are relevant if you are receiving Incapacity Benefit, contribution-based ESA, JSA or other benefits that are taxable.

The final section on page TR3 is for reporting other UK income not included on the supplementary pages and, in most cases, is unlikely to be relevant to your circumstances.

Page TR4 is devoted to tax reliefs, the first part of which is relevant if you want to claim relief for pension contributions. It is likely that the only boxes you will need to complete are Boxes 1 and 2.

## Figure 14.4

**Paying into registered pension schemes and overseas pension schemes**

Do not include payments you make to your employer's pension scheme which are deducted from your pay before tax or payments made by your employer. If your contributions and other pension inputs are more than the Annual Allowance, you should also fill in boxes 10, 11 and 12 on page Ai 4 of the 'Additional information' pages.

1  Payments to registered pension schemes where basic rate tax relief will be claimed by your pension provider (called 'relief at source'). Enter the payments and basic rate tax

£ 4400 · 00

2  Payments to a retirement annuity contract where basic rate tax relief will not be claimed by your provider

£ 1800 · 00

3  Payments to your employer's scheme which were not deducted from your pay before tax - this will be unusual - read the notes

£           · 00

4  Payments to an overseas pension scheme, which is not UK-registered, which are eligible for tax relief and were not deducted from your pay before tax

£           · 00

**SOURCE** HMRC

If you pay tax at the higher or additional rates you will be entitled to tax relief on the difference between either 40 per cent or 45 per cent and the basic rate of 20 per cent on your donations to charities under Gift Aid. However, even if you are not claiming this tax relief you should complete the part of the Return on charitable giving as follows.

- The total of all your Gift Aid payments goes in Box 5.
- In Box 6 you need to enter the total of any 'one-off' payments in the figure in Box 5.
- Any Gift Aid donations made in 2024/25 and related back to 2023/24 go in Box 7.
- Perhaps by the time you fill in your Tax Return and send it back to your tax office you have made donations under Gift Aid in the 2024/25 tax year. You can elect to have those payments treated as though they were made in the year to 5 April 2024. Enter the figure in Box 8. Again, do this on the first tax return and do not amend it. Always ensure your filings are accurate and please leave time for thorough checks.
- The value of any shares or securities, land and buildings that you have gifted to charity in the year should be entered in Boxes 9 and 10 respectively.

In Boxes 11 and 12 you should respectively state:

- the value of any investments gifted to non-UK charities in Boxes 9 and 10; and
- Gift Aid payments to non-UK charities in Box 5.

## Figure 14.5

The next tax relief section on page TR4 is only of relevance to you if you can make a claim for the special blind person's allowance. You need to give the name of the local authority, or equivalent body, with whom you have registered your blindness.

## Figure 14.6

Page TR5 is concerned with:

- Student Loan repayments;
- High Income Child Benefit Charge; and
- the Marriage Allowance.

You will only need to complete the High Income Child Benefit Charge section if:

- your income was over £60,000 in 2024/25;
- you or your spouse/partner received Child Benefit in the year to 5 April 2024; and
- for couples only – your income was more than that of your spouse/partner.

**Figure 14.7**

### Marriage Allowance

Please read the notes. If your income for the year ended 5 April 2025 was less than £12,570 you can transfer £1,260 of your Personal Allowance to your spouse or civil partner to reduce the amount of tax they pay if all of the following apply:
- you were married to, or in a civil partnership with, the same person for all or part of the tax year
- you were both born on or after 6 April 1935
- your spouse or civil partner's income was not taxed at the higher rate

Fill in this section if you want to make the transfer:

| 1 Your spouse or civil partner's first name | 4 Your spouse or civil partner's date of birth DD MM YYYY |
|---|---|
| TOM | 06 08 1952 |

| 2 Your spouse or civil partner's last name | 5 Date of marriage or civil partnership DD MM YYYY |
|---|---|
| SMITH | 19 05 1978 |

| 3 Your spouse or civil partner's National Insurance number |
|---|
| BZ 62 24 17 A |

**SOURCE** HMRC

Perhaps your income in 2024/25 was under £12,570? If so, you can cut the tax bill of your spouse/partner by transferring £1,260 of your personal allowance to them. But to do so all of the following must apply.

- You were both born after 5 April 1935.
- You were married to, or in a civil partnership with, the same person for all or part of 2023/24.
- The income of your spouse or civil partner in 2023/24 was no more than £50,270.

## Figure 14.8

### High Income Child Benefit Charge

Fill in this section if all of the following apply:
- your income was over £50,000
- you or your partner (if you have one) got Child Benefit (this also applies if someone else claims Child Benefit for a child who lives with you and pays you or your partner for the child's upkeep)
- couples only - your income was higher than your partner's

Please read the notes. Use the calculator at www.gov.uk/child-benefit-tax-calculator to help you work out the Child Benefit payments you received.

If you have to pay this charge for the 2023–24 tax year and you do not want us to use your 2023–24 PAYE tax code to collect that tax during the year, put 'X' in box 3 on page TR 6.

1. Enter the total amount of Child Benefit you and your partner got for the year to 5 April 2024

   1788.00

2. Enter the number of children you and your partner got Child Benefit for on 5 April 2024

   2

3. Enter the date that you and your partner stopped getting all Child Benefit payments if this was before 6 April 2024
   DD MM YYYY

**SOURCE** HMRC

Before you finish off your Tax Return, you should look at the Additional Information pages, which are for less common types of income, and other tax reliefs and information.

In particular, the second section on page Ai2 is for you to claim other tax reliefs, such as the following.

- Your subscriptions for new ordinary shares in a VCT go in Box 1.
- Box 2 is for your subscriptions for shares issued under the Enterprise EIS.
- The total of your qualifying loan interest payable in the year should be entered in Box 5.
- Maintenance or alimony payments you are making, subject to a maximum of £4,280, should be entered in Box 7, but only if you or your former spouse or civil partner was born before 6 April 1935.
- In Box 10 you should put the amount of your subscriptions for shares under the SEIS.

## Figure 14.9

**Other tax reliefs** – read the notes

| | | | |
|---|---|---|---|
| 1 | Subscriptions for Venture Capital Trust shares - the amount on which relief is claimed<br>£ 4000·00 | 7 | Maintenance payments (up to £3,530) - if you or your former spouse or civil partner were born before 6 April 1935<br>£ 2810·00 |
| 2 | Subscriptions for shares under the Enterprise Investment Scheme - the amount on which relief is claimed<br>£ 2920·00 | 8 | Payments to a trade union for death benefits - half the amount paid (maximum £100)<br>£ ·00 |
| 3 | Community Investment Tax Relief - the amount on which relief is claimed<br>£ ·00 | 9 | Relief claimed on a qualifying distribution on the redemption of bonus shares or securities<br>£ ·00 |
| 4 | Annual payments made<br>£ ·00 | 10 | Subscriptions for shares under the Seed Enterprise Investment Scheme<br>£ 1340·00 |
| 5 | Qualifying loan interest payable in the year<br>£ 830·00 | 11 | Social Investment Tax Relief - the amount on which relief is claimed<br>£ ·00 |
| 6 | Post-cessation trade relief and certain other losses<br>£ ·00 | 12 | Non-deductible loan interest from investments into property partnerships not included in box 5<br>£ ·00 |

**SOURCE** HMRC

Then follows a section on the married couple's allowance. You should carefully read the notes at the top of page Ai3 before completing Boxes 1 to 11 as appropriate.

The second part of this page is devoted to Income Tax losses and the limit of Income Tax relief on these losses (see Chapter 7).

You are probably now in a position to put the finishing touches to your Tax Return. If you want to calculate your tax you will have to ask HMRC for the Tax Calculation Summary, notes and helpsheets that will assist you in working out any tax due or repayable, and if payments on account are necessary.

There is a choice of boxes to complete on page TR6 if you have not paid enough tax.

- Box 2 covers tax due for 2023/24 and the alternative methods of payment if you owe less than £3,000.
- Box 3 deals with the collection of tax for 2024/25 on your savings income and/or the High Income Child Benefit Charge.

But if you have overpaid you need to give the information requested in Boxes 4 to 14 on page TR6 of the bank or building society account into which you would like the tax refund paid.

Do not miss the deadline for filing your Tax Return because, perhaps, you are waiting for some final figures. Use estimates and make sure you send the correct figures as soon as you can. You should tick Box 20 on page TR8 of your Return and describe in the space provided at Box 19:

- which figures are provisional (you should refer to the appropriate box numbers on your Tax Return or any other supplementary pages you have completed);
- why you could not give final figures; and
- when you expect to be able to provide your tax office with the correct information.

Put 'X' in Box 21 if you are enclosing separate supplementary pages. You must then sign and date the Return in Box 22. Have regard to the wording of the declaration:

> I declare the information I've given on this tax return and any supplementary pages is correct and complete to the best of my knowledge and belief. I understand that I may have to pay financial penalties and face prosecution if I give false information.

The form and any supplementary pages are now ready to send back to your tax office.

## Working out your tax

The key steps in calculating your tax bill are as follows.

1. Add up all the non-savings income you have entered on your Return.
2. Total the allowances and other deductions you have claimed for the year but excluding those such as personal pension premiums and donations under Gift Aid paid net of tax at the basic rate.
3. Take (2) away from (1).
4. Work out the tax due on (3) but increasing the basic rate band of £37,700 by the grossed up equivalent of personal pension and Gift Aid payments.

**5** Add up your savings income for the year. Take into account the Personal Savings Allowance and calculate the tax on the balance.

**6** Do the same for your dividend income, not forgetting the dividend allowance.

**7** Add (4), (5) and (6) together.

**8** If you are self-employed or in partnership, work out how much you owe for 4 National Insurance Contributions.

**9** Add (7) and (8) together and take away all tax deducted at source.

This is your tax bill unless you also owe tax on capital gains realized in excess of your annual exemption limit. You will then be able to:

- work out what tax you have to pay for 2024/25 due on 31 January 2026; and
- calculate any payments on account for 2025/26 payable on 31 January and 31 July 2026.

## Illustration

Celia Mercer, who is single, is employed as a fashion designer. She frequently has to travel so her employer provides her with a company car, fuel for private mileage as well as private medical insurance cover.

In her spare time Celia speaks at trade shows. She also writes articles for fashion magazines.

A few years ago Celia's mother died. The inheritance she received is invested in a portfolio of shares. She also owns a buy-to-let flat and has spare cash deposited in building society accounts.

Celia files her Tax Return for the year to 5 April 2024 online on 24 November 2024. It shows the following entries:

| Tax calculation for 2023–24 | |
|---|---:|
| Pay from all employments | £64,000.00 |
| *plus* benefits and expenses received | £9,914.00 |
| **Total from all employments** | £73,914.00 |
| Profit from self-employment | £9,940.00 |

*(continued)*

## How to complete your Tax Return and work out your tax

*(Continued)*

| | |
|---|---:|
| Profit from UK land and property | £4,500.00 |
| Interest from UK banks, building societies and securities etc | £1,200.00 |
| Dividends from UK companies | £1,620.00 |
| Total income received | £91,174.00 |
| *minus* Personal Allowance | £12,570.00 |
| Total income on which tax is due | £78,604.00 |

### How we have worked out your income tax

Your basic rate limit has been increased by £2,750.00 to £40,450.00 for pension payments.

This reduces the amount of income charged to higher rates of tax.

| | Amount | Percentage | Total |
|---|---:|---:|---:|
| **Pay, pensions, profit etc (UK rate for England and Northern Ireland)** | | | |
| Basic rate | £40,450.00 | x 20% | £8,090.00 |
| Higher rate | £35,334.00 | x 40% | £14,133.60 |
| Savings interest from banks or building societies, securities etc | | | |
| Higher rate band at nil rate | £500.00 | x 0% | £0.00 |
| Higher rate | £700.00 | x 40% | £280.00 |
| Dividends from companies etc | | | |
| Basic rate | £0.00 | x 8.75% | £0.00 |
| Higher rate at nil rate | £1,000.00 | x 0% | £0.00 |
| Higher rate | £620.00 | x 33.75% | £209.25 |
| Income Tax due after allowances and reliefs | | | £22,712.85 |
| *minus* Relief for finance costs | £3,100.00 | x 20% | £620.00 |

*(continued)*

*(Continued)*

|  | Amount | Percentage | Total |
|---|---|---|---|
| Income Tax due after tax reductions | £22,092.85 |  |  |
| Income Tax due | £22,092.85 |  |  |
| If you've registered for Class 2 NICs, your contributions have been treated as paid |  |  |  |
| Your Class 2 National Insurance contributions due are | £0.00 |  |  |
| Income Tax due after allowances and reliefs |  |  | £22,092.85 |
| *minus* Tax deducted |  |  |  |
| From all employments, UK pensions and state benefits | £18,240.00 |  |  |
| Total tax deducted | £18,240.00 |  |  |
| Total Income Tax due |  |  | £3,852.85 |
| Taxable Capital Gains | £2,600.00 |  |  |
| Other gains | £2,600.00 | x 20% | £520.00 |
| Capital Gains Tax due | £520.00 |  |  |
| Income and Capital Gains Tax due |  |  | £4,372.85 |
| Less payments on account |  |  |  |
| 31 January 2024 |  |  | £1,200.00 |
| 31 July 2024 |  |  | £1,200.00 |
| 2023–24 balancing payment |  |  | £1,972.85 |
| Total due by 31 January 2025 |  |  | £1,972.85 |

# What HMRC do

When your completed Tax Return is received by your tax office it will be processed as quickly as possible based on your entries on the Return. Any simple straightforward mistakes will be corrected by HMRC and you will be told about them.

You will then be sent a calculation of your tax position if you have asked HMRC to work this out for you. Alternatively, if you have calculated your own tax bill and it is incorrect, HMRC will send you their tax calculation.

## Some other hints on efficient tax compliance

### Tax Saver

Always remember that both send-back dates of 31 October (for paper) and 31 January (online) are critical. You must stick to them otherwise you will come within the penalty regime for the late filing of the Return.

### Tax Saver

If the amount of any of your sources of income is substantially different compared to the previous year, use the Additional Information box on page TR7 to explain the reason for the change.

### Tax Saver

Do not forget to sign the Return. This is one of the most common mistakes that HMRC have found when processing Tax Returns.

> **Tax Saver**
>
> Remember that you can amend your Self Assessment at any time in the 12-month period after the latest 31 January deadline.

> **Tax Saver**
>
> Remember the key dates in the Self Assessment calendar, which are summarized in Appendix 7.

# 15
# Paying your tax, interest and penalties

Under the Self Assessment tax system:

- there are specified dates each year when you must pay your tax; and
- you regularly receive a Statement of Account from HMRC detailing both tax recently paid and the next amount due.

## Tax payment dates

The tax payment dates for 2024/25 are:

|  |  | Due date for tax payments on account | Due date for final balance |
|---|---|---|---|
| Rental income and untaxed investment income |  |  |  |
| Business profits | 50% | 31/1/2025 | 31/1/2026 |
| Unpaid PAYE (where not coded) | 50% | 31/1/2025 |  |
| Higher and additional rate tax on investment income (taxed at source) |  |  |  |
| Capital Gains Tax |  | N/A | 31/1/2026 |

The one exception to the rule requiring direct payment of tax to HMRC relates to employees or pensioners who owe less than £3,000 in tax. They can choose to have the amount collected monthly in the following year through the PAYE system:

- by filing a paper Return at their tax office no later than 31 October following the end of the tax year; or
- by filing online by 30 December after the end of the tax year.

## Payments on account

Some taxpayers, mainly those who are self-employed, will make two payments on account of the tax due for a year on:

- 31 January in the tax year; and
- 31 July following the end of the tax year.

Payments on account are worked out by splitting into two equal amounts the tax paid for the previous tax year (after taking off tax incurred at source and any Capital Gains Tax).

You do not need to make payments on account of Income Tax if:

- the amount you owe for Income Tax and Class 4 National Insurance Contributions for the previous tax year, after taking off tax paid at source, is less than £1,000; or
- at least 80 per cent of your Income Tax and Class 4 National Insurance Contributions bill for the preceding tax year was represented by tax deducted from the income before you received it.

It follows that most employees and pensioners will not have to make the half-yearly payments on account.

## Reduced payments on account

Maybe, because of a change in your financial circumstances, your payments on account for the tax year (based on what you paid in the previous year) point towards an overstatement of your likely liability for the year.

This might happen where you expect:

- your income in 2025/26 to be lower than that in 2024/25; or
- your allowances or reliefs to be higher; or
- that more of your income will incur tax at source, for example under PAYE, in 2024/25.

# Paying your tax, interest and penalties

> **Tax Saver**
>
> In such circumstances you can claim to reduce your payments on account. You do this by using Form SA303, which is available online or from your tax office. The form gives guidance on how to complete it.

If the claim to reduce your payments on account subsequently turns out to be excessive then you will be asked to pay interest on the difference between the reduced tax you actually paid and the payments on account that should have been made.

## Statements of Account

At the top of your Self Assessment Statement you will see:

- the Statement number and date of issue;
- your 10-digit UTR;
- your NINO; and
- your employer's tax reference, if you are employed.

The Statement then goes on to document:

- the opening balance, if any, brought forward from the previous Statement;
- what has happened since the last Statement; and
- whether there is an over-payment or, most probably, an amount to pay, and when to pay it. This is shown in a summary box at the end of the Statement.

Payments on account are payments towards your next year's Income Tax. The amount you have to pay for each payment on account is half of your previous year's tax bill.

Payments on account are due on 31 January during the tax year, and 31 July soon after its end. For example, on 31 January 2025 and 31 July 2025 you may be told to make payments on account towards the tax that you're going to have to pay on your income for the 2024/25 tax year, even though the Tax Return for that year is not due until 31 January 2026.

If you end up paying too much, HMRC will give you the difference back, either via cheque or bank transfer or by deducting the difference from your next tax bill.

The self-assessment calculation of the balancing payment does not take into account payments on account made and that you can deduct both payments in determining the tax due on 31 January.

You should also receive a Statement of Account whenever there is a change to the amount of tax you owe, and where you are due a refund from HMRC.

Other points of interest are:

- As HMRC carry out security checks, any tax refund due to you may not actually be issued until some time after the date shown on your Statement of Account.
- Where a tax liability will shortly be due for payment, HMRC will usually set any tax refund against this amount and then just repay the balance.
- If you have made a payment in the short period before you receive a Statement, it will appear on the next one.

If you have a Personal Tax Account or have registered for Self Assessment online you can access a wide range of services, including:

- viewing the latest issued copy of your Statement, as well as any Statements issued to you in the last three years;
- viewing payments/credits and how these have been allocated;
- viewing liabilities by tax year, including interest, penalties and surcharges;
- requesting repayments where an account is in credit;
- claiming to reduce payments on account;
- viewing and changing your address; and
- paying by direct debit online.

## Paying your tax

There are a number of secure and efficient methods for paying your tax recommended by HMRC.

You can pay online, over the phone or by bank transfer. Direct debit is also an option.

## Paying your tax, interest and penalties

Many of us:

- already use direct debit to make regular payments for household and other costs; and
- are familiar with the advantages of paying by direct debit.

Under the Budget Payment Plan, which is voluntary, you can make regular payments towards a future tax liability. The plan is flexible and you:

- decide the regular weekly or monthly amount you want to pay to HMRC;
- can choose to amend your regular payment amount;
- are free to take a break or suspend payment for a period of up to six months; and
- can cancel the Budget Payment Plan at any time.

The payments you make are in advance, and reduce what you have to pay on either the following 31 January or 31 July.

You must still pay the full amount of tax by the due date.

If you use payment by post you should:

- make your cheque out to 'HM Revenue & Customs Only' followed by your Unique Taxpayer Reference; and
- send it to HMRC in the return envelope accompanied by the tear-off payment slip from your Statement of Account.

A stamp for the correct postage is needed. If you do not have a return envelope, your cheque should be sent to HMRC, Direct BX5 5BD.

HMRC politely request that:

- your cheque and the tear-off payment slip be unfolded;
- you do not staple or attach paperclips to cheques; and
- you do not pay your tax by sending cash through the post.

You can assist your accounts office in dealing promptly with your tax payment by:

- including a separate letter if you are sending a post-dated cheque, or want to give further information about your payment; and
- paying on time – you will not then incur interest charges.

## Business Payment Support Service

The Payment Support Service is dedicated to assisting businesses with temporary cash flow problems. If you are concerned about being able to meet tax, National Insurance or other payments due to HMRC or that future payments could cause you difficulties, you can get in touch with HMRC to discuss payment options. You will be asked for the following information: your tax reference number, details of the tax that you are having or will have trouble paying, and an outline summary of the income and expenses of your business.

This will enable HMRC staff to review your particular circumstances and discuss temporary options relevant to the needs of your business, which could, for example, include allowing you to make tax payments over a longer period. You will not be charged late payment surcharges in such an arrangement although interest will continue to accrue on payments made beyond their due and payable date.

The number to telephone if you need assistance is 0300 200 3835.

## What if I can't pay my tax?

If you are unable to settle your tax bill you should speak to the office which sent you the most recent communication. They should be able to help you by giving you extra time to pay, or allowing you to settle it in installments.

HMRC has several options when you fail to either reach an agreement, or maintain the payments you said you would make.

These are:

- collecting what you owe through your earnings or pension;
- taking money from either your bank or building society account;
- seizing possessions for sale at auction;
- magistrates or County Court proceedings; or
- making you bankrupt.

## Date of receipt

Tax payments are considered to be received by the accounts office as follows:

| Payment method | Effective date of payment |
|---|---|
| Received by post (except below) | Day of receipt by HMRC |
| Received by post following a day when the office has been closed for whatever reason (including a weekend) | The day the office was first closed (for payments received on Monday, the effective date will be the previous Saturday) |
| Electronic Funds Transfer – payment by BACS or CHAPS | One working day immediately before the date that the value is received (a working day is defined as a Bank of England working day) |
| Bank Giro | The date on which payment was made at the bank |

# Interest

You will be charged late payment interest if you do not pay your tax when it is due, and on any penalties based on the overdue tax.

The interest is calculated from the date on which the tax becomes due and payable until payment is made.

At the time of writing the late payment rate is 7.50 per cent from 20 August 2024. Tax relief on the interest is not allowed. Please note that from April 2025, the interest rate on unpaid tax liabilities charged by HMRC will increase by 1.5 per cent.

There may be circumstances when the imposition of interest would not be fair to you and can be justifiably contested. HMRC's Code of Practice (No 1) sets out the circumstances in which HMRC will consider setting aside a change to interest in overdue tax where there has been an undue delay on their part.

You will be paid interest, which is called repayment interest and is not taxable, by HMRC on overpayment of any of the following:

- payments on account of Income Tax;
- Income Tax and Capital Gains Tax; and
- any penalties imposed.

The formula for working out the interest rate on repayments is Bank Base Rate minus 1 per cent but with a minimum rate of 0.5 per cent.

## Remission of tax

Arrears of Income Tax or Capital Gains Tax may be waived if they result from HMRC's failure to make proper and timely use of information from the following sources:

- The taxpayer about his or her own income, capital gains or personal circumstances.
- An employer, where the information affects an employee's notice of coding.
- The DWP about a taxpayer's retirement, disability or widow's State Pension.

The concession is normally only given where the taxpayer could reasonably have believed that his or her tax affairs were in order, and is notified of the arrears by the end of the tax year following that in which it arose.

## Late payment penalty

A late payment penalty is levied on the late payment of Income Tax, but not payments on account, or Capital Gains Tax as follows:

| | |
|---|---|
| Tax unpaid by 3 March* (30 days after the tax was due) | 5% of unpaid tax |
| Tax unpaid by 3 August* (5 months after the initial penalty was imposed) | Further 5% of tax unpaid |
| Tax unpaid by 3 February* (11 months after the initial penalty was imposed) | Further 5% of tax unpaid |

*These dates will be one day earlier when 31 January falls in a leap year.

A penalty notice must be formally served on you by HMRC. You have 30 days in which to appeal against the notice if you think you have a reasonable excuse for the late payment of the tax. Your appeal might be successful:

- if there is clear evidence that your cheque was lost in the post; or
- in the event of serious illness.

Examples of circumstances where your appeal will be rejected are cheques wrongly made out, and lack of funds other than for exceptional reasons.

# Penalties

The main penalties under Self Assessment are:

| Offence | Penalty |
| --- | --- |
| You do not submit a paper Tax Return to your tax office by 31 October after the end of the tax year | £100 |
| You do not file online by 31 January after the end of the tax year | £100 |
| Your Return is more than three months late | An automatic penalty of £10 a day up to a maximum of £900 |
| Your Return is more than six months late | A tax geared penalty that is the greater of 5% of the tax due and £300 |
| Your Return is still outstanding after a year | Another tax geared penalty that again is the greater of 5% of the tax due and £300 |
| | In particularly serious cases a higher penalty of up to 100% of the tax due can be imposed. |

It is important to note that the time limits for the imposition of these late filing penalties run from:

- 31 October for paper Returns; and
- 31 January for online filers.

Where taxpayers have a genuinely good excuse for missing the annual filing deadline for submitting Tax Returns, they can appeal against the automatic late filing penalty.

What may be accepted by HMRC as a reasonable excuse for late filing include:

- where the Tax Return was not received by the taxpayer;
- where the Tax Return was lost in the post or delayed because of:
  - a fire or flood at the post office where the Tax Return was handled;
  - prolonged industrial action within the post office; or
  - an unforeseen event that disrupted the postal services.

- where a taxpayer lost his or her tax records as a result of fire, flood or theft;
- serious illness; and
- death of a spouse, domestic partner or close relative.

HMRC will not agree the following as a reasonable excuse for being late:

- Tax Return too difficult;
- pressure of work;
- lack of information; or
- absence of reminders from HMRC.

The other penalties are:

| Offence | Penalty |
| --- | --- |
| You do not receive a Tax Return and fail to notify HMRC of chargeability to tax within six months of the end of the tax year | Percentage of the tax payable:<br>a) None if the failure is not deliberate<br>b) 30% for a careless oversight<br>c) 70% for a deliberate but not concealed failure<br>d) 100% if the failure was both deliberate and concealed |
| Failure to maintain and keep records | Up to £3,000 |
| Fraudulently or negligently claiming to reduce interim tax payments | Up to an amount equivalent to the difference between the tax paid and the tax that should have been paid |

Generally, a penalty determination must be made, or proceedings commenced, within six years of the date on which the penalty was incurred. The rules allow for this period of time to be extended to any later date within three years of the final determination of the tax liability.

The penalty regime for errors on documents and Returns depends on why you made the error, and how serious the reason was.

HMRC use penalties to stop individuals who do not take care with their tax affairs from gaining an unfair advantage. If you take reasonable care to get it right, HMRC will not charge a penalty where an error occurs. Some of the ways you can demonstrate you took reasonable care are:

- Keeping accurate records and updating them regularly so you can make sure your Tax Returns are correct.
- Saving your records should you need them at a later date.

- Checking what the correct position is when you do not understand something or, alternatively, seeking advice from HMRC or a competent tax adviser.
- Telling HMRC as soon as possible about any error you discover after sending in a Tax Return or other document.

If you do not take reasonable care HMRC can penalize any errors, and penalties will be higher if the errors are deliberate.

What if you have to pay a penalty? HMRC will:

- Contact you to discuss your tax.
- Discuss the reason for the error – the more serious the reason, the higher the tax penalty can be.
- Reduce the penalty if you help them work out the correct tax due.
- Explain why they are issuing a penalty and send you a penalty notice. HMRC can substantially reduce any penalty due if you:
    - tell them about any errors without being prompted;
    - help them work out if any extra tax is due; and
    - allow them to check your figures.

The penalty is a percentage of the extra tax due and depends on why you made the error, as follows:

| Reason | Rate of penalty Maximum | Rate of penalty Minimum |
|---|---|---|
| Lack of reasonable care | 30% | 0% |
| Deliberate | 70% | 20% |
| Deliberate and concealed | 100% | 30% |

You will have to pay the tax and any interest due, as well as the penalty.

If you incur a penalty because you failed to take reasonable care with your tax affairs, HMRC can suspend it for up to two years. In that time you need to get your systems right. If you then meet all the conditions laid down by HMRC the penalty will be cancelled.

You always have the right of appeal where you think that a penalty is unfair.

# 16
# Elections and claims: time limits

You will already have gathered that certain options available to you as a taxpayer are dependent on you submitting an election or making a claim to HMRC. As these will usually involve a saving in tax it is important to appreciate that you often need to act within prescribed time limits. This chapter brings together those elections and claims that are most likely to be of relevance to you. It also sets out the time limit for submission to HMRC. It is by no means exhaustive.

## *Chapter 2 – Tax rates and allowances*

| Election/claim | Time limit |
| --- | --- |
| The various elections for the transfer of the married couple's and blind person's allowances | Generally, before the start of the tax year for which it is to have effect |
| Claim to the personal allowances detailed in the chapter | No later than four years after 31 January next following the end of the tax year |
| Transfer of excess allowances between spouses/civil partners | No later than four years after 31 January next following the end of the tax year |

## *Chapter 3 – Tax credits*

| Election/claim | Time limit |
| --- | --- |
| Claims for tax credits | Claims will only be backdated by a maximum of one month |
| Annual renewal | By 31 July following the end of a tax year |

## Chapter 4 – Interest payments and other outgoings

| Election/claim | Time limit |
| --- | --- |
| Election to treat charity donations under Gift Aid as made in the previous tax year | On or before when you deliver your Tax Return for the previous year after the tax year |

## Chapter 6 – Value Added Tax

| Election/claim | Time limit |
| --- | --- |
| Application for registration | No later than 30 days from the end of the month after the one when turnover exceeds the registration limit |
| Claim for bad debt relief | When a debt remains unpaid for more than six months |

## Chapter 7 – Working for yourself

| Election/claim | Time limit |
| --- | --- |
| Cash accounting for a small business | Tick box on page SEF1 of the Tax Return |
| £1,000 small business income allowance | No later than one year after 31 January next following the tax year for the claim |
| Relief for post-cessation expenses | No later than one year after 31 January next following the tax year in which the payments are made |
| Creating a separate pool to work out the capital allowances on an asset with a short life expectancy | No later than one year after 31 January next following the tax year in which the period of account ended in which the expenditure is incurred |
| Relief for the loss sustained in the tax year against other income of the same year or the preceding year | Within one year after 31 January next following the tax year in which the loss arose |
| Relief for a trading loss against the profits arising from the same trade in subsequent periods | Within four years after 31 January next following the tax year in which the loss was sustained |

*(continued)*

*(Continued)*

| Election/claim | Time limit |
|---|---|
| Relief for the loss in the first four years of assessment of a new business to be given against the income of the three preceding years of assessment | No later than one year after 31 January next following the tax year in which the loss occurred |
| Relief for trading losses to be offset against capital gains | No later than one year after 31 January next following the tax year |
| Relief for the loss in the last 12 months of trading to be given against the profits of the same trade that were assessed in the three tax years prior to the year in which the trade was discontinued | Within four years after 31 January next following the tax year in which the trade ceased |

## Chapter 10 – Savings and investment income

| Election/claim | Time limit |
|---|---|
| To claim a repayment of tax on your savings income | Within four years after the end of the tax year for which you are claiming |
| £1,000 small property income allowance | No later than one year after 31 January next following the tax year for the claim |
| An election to opt out of rent-a-room relief for a particular tax year, or withdrawal of an election | Within one year after 31 January next following the tax year |
| An election for the alternative basis of rent-a-room relief, or revocation of an election | Within one year after 31 January next following the tax year |
| Claim for Income Tax relief under the Enterprise Investment Scheme | Within four years after 31 January next following that in which the shares were issued |
| Claim for Income Tax relief under the Seed Enterprise Investment Scheme | Within four years after 31 January next following that in which the shares were issued |
| Declaration by a married couple or civil partners that their beneficial interest in joint property and the income arising from it are unequal | The date of the declaration, which must be sent to HMRC within 60 days |

## Chapter 13 – Capital gains

| Election/claim | Time limit |
| --- | --- |
| Claim to the capital loss where the value of an asset becomes negligible | The loss arises on the date of claim although, in practice, a two-year period is allowed from the end of the tax year in which the asset became of negligible value |
| Claim for the loss on shares that were originally subscribed for in an unquoted trading company to be set against income in the year of loss, or the preceding year | No later than one year after 31 January next following the tax year in which the loss was made |
| Claim to Business Asset Disposal Relief | No later than one year after 31 January next following the tax year in which the disposal took place |
| An election to determine which of your homes is to be regarded as your principal residence for Capital Gains Tax purposes | Two years from the date when two or more properties are eligible |

# 17
# Inheritance Tax

Inheritance Tax is payable on:

- any chargeable transfers you make during your lifetime; and
- the value of your estate on death.

The current rate of inheritance tax is 40 per cent, but business property relief and agriculture property relief with assets over £1m command a rate of zero per cent. This is changing, however, and rising to 20 per cent from April 2026 after the first £1m.

There are a number of exemptions and reliefs that, if optimized, can reduce the amount of tax payable, perhaps significantly.

As with all types of direct taxation, husband, wife and civil partners are all treated as separate individuals.

Inheritance Tax is administered by the Inheritance Tax Office of HMRC on 0300 123 1072, to whom all Returns and Accounts should be submitted.

Some of the aspects of the tax are complex, particularly those relating to agricultural and business property and transfers into Trusts.

Like many taxes, there is a threshold for Inheritance Tax and until 2030 this is frozen at £325,000 per individual. This can help people protect much of their estate from Inheritance Tax. For example, if an estate was worth £335,000, then Inheritance Tax would only be chargeable on the additional £10,000 above this threshold. This is also known as the nil-rate band.

What follows is a summary of the main areas of the tax that are likely to be of most relevance and interest to you.

## Rates of tax payable

On your death Inheritance Tax is payable on:

- the net value of your estate immediately before your demise; and
- any PET or CLT made in the previous seven years.

The amount of Inheritance Tax payable is determined by the following table:

| Cumulative chargeable transfers (£) | Rate (%) |
| --- | --- |
| 0–325,000 | 0 |
| Over 325,000 | 40 |

The tax due on each chargeable gift or the value of your estate on death is dependent upon the cumulative value of all other chargeable transfers in the previous seven years. Importantly, the rate of Inheritance Tax chargeable can fall to 36 per cent if 10 per cent or more of the estate's net value is left to charity.

## Potentially exempt transfers

Perhaps the most significant feature of Inheritance Tax is that of a potentially exempt transfer (PET). This is:

- an outright gift to an individual;
- a gift into settlement for the benefit of a disabled person; or
- certain other transfers into Trust.

No tax is payable providing the donor survives for at least seven years from the date of making the gift.

## Chargeable lifetime gifts

Any gift or transfer that is not potentially exempt is liable to Inheritance Tax when it is made. Typically, a gift into settlement is a chargeable lifetime transfer (CLT). In working out any Inheritance Tax due at the date of gift:

- it is only the excess, if any, over the nil rate band on which tax is payable; and
- the rate of tax is one-half of the rate applicable on death at the time.

## Gifts with reservation and pre-owned assets

If you make a gift but carry on enjoying some benefit from the property or asset, it is still likely to be regarded as yours until either:

- the date when you stop enjoying any benefit from the gift; or
- your death.

This is what is known as a 'gift with reservation'.

You also have to pay Income Tax each year on the value of any assets that you continue to use or enjoy after you have given them away.

# Exemptions

The main exemptions for individuals are:

- Transfers, without limit, between spouses/civil partners – both during lifetime and on death.
- Gifts up to £3,000 in any one tax year. Any part of the exemption that is unused can be carried forward, but to the following year only.

---

Nancy Young gave her brother £1,800 in August 2023. A year later, she wanted to make a more substantial gift, but this time to her sister. She was able to give away £4,200 in September 2024, within her annual exemption limits for 2023/24 and 2024/25 as follows:

|  | £ |
|---|---|
| **2023/24** | |
| Annual exemption limit | 3,000 |
| *Less*: Gift to brother | 1,800 |
| Carried forward to next year | 1,200 |
| **2024/25** | |
| Annual exemption limit | 3,000 |
| *Add*: Exemption unused in 2023/24 | 1,200 |
| Available exemption for the year | 4,200 |
| Gift to sister | 4,200 |

If Nancy had given her brother £3,000 in August 2023, she would have been limited to gifting the same amount to her sister in 2024/25.

> **Tax Saver**
>
> Using your annual exemption can save £1,200 of Inheritance Tax each year (£3,000 × 40 per cent). A couple can save £2,400 a year. Over a period of 10 years, for example, this amounts to a £12,000 reduction in the tax payable on your death, increasing to £24,000 for a couple.

- Gifts to any number of persons, but only up to £250 per person in each tax year. Where the total amount given to any one individual exceeds the amount of £250 then no part of the gift comes within the exemption.
- Marriage gifts. The amount you can give away in consideration of marriage or civil partnership depends on your relationship to the bride, groom or civil partner, as follows:

|  | £ |
| --- | --- |
| By either parent | 5,000 |
| By a grandparent or great grandparent | 2,500 |
| By any other person | 1,000 |

- Regular gifts out of income that form part of your normal expenditure. You need to be able to demonstrate that:
    - taking one year with another your regular gifts came out of income; and
    - you were left with sufficient income to maintain your usual lifestyle.

> **Tax Saver**
>
> Glyn Fielding, who lives alone, has an annual after-tax income of around £30,000. He has a modest lifestyle. He spends about £20,000 a year on his home, food, recreation, holidays and other living expenses.
>
> His brother, Luke, who is married, is not so fortunate. Glyn could make regular gifts to his brother out of his annual surplus income of £10,000, free of Inheritance Tax.
>
> Over 10 years Glyn might save £40,000 in Inheritance Tax.

- Lifetime gifts and bequests on death to charities and 'qualifying' political parties, without limit.

# Your home

These days many of us feel an increasing need during our lifetime to help our children meet the costs of university or other further education, and, later on in life, towards a deposit on a home.

Perhaps you can only look to your home, where the greatest part of your wealth is tied up, as a source of funds to help your children? But how and what you do with your home has ramifications for Inheritance Tax. If:

- you gift your home and move out you can come back to visit or make short stays without incurring an Inheritance Tax charge;
- you give your home away but continue to live there you must pay the new owner a commercial rent in order to avoid Inheritance Tax;
- you sell your home, then whatever amount from the sale proceeds you give to your children will be outside of Inheritance Tax provided you survive for seven years from the date of the gift (but if you then move in with them you will be exposed to an Income Tax charge on a 'pre-owned asset'); or
- you give your home to your children and they move in with you, you will not have avoided Inheritance Tax as this will count as a 'gift with reservation of benefit'.

For couples, how you own your home determines the way in which it is passed on when you die, as follows:

| Ownership | Beneficiary |
| --- | --- |
| Joint tenancy between spouses or civil partners | The survivor, automatically |
| Tenancy in common | In accordance with the Will of the deceased, his or her share can be divided between the surviving spouse, partner and their children |

# Business property

Transfers in lifetime or on death, subject to certain conditions, of eligible business assets and interests in businesses qualify for relief from Inheritance Tax. There are two rates:

- 100 per cent for:
  - unincorporated businesses;
  - all holdings of unquoted shares in qualifying companies.
- 50 per cent for:
  - shares giving control of a quoted company;
  - land, buildings, machinery or plant used in a partnership or controlled company where the transferor is a partner or controlling shareholder.

From 6 April 2026, the treatment of business property under Inheritance Tax is being reformed.

In addition to existing nil-rate bands and exemptions, the current 100 per cent rates of relief will continue for the first £1 million of business property to help protect family businesses.

The rate of relief will be 50 per cent thereafter, and in all circumstances for quoted shares designated as 'not listed' on the markets of recognized stock exchanges, such as AIM.

## Agricultural property

The reliefs applying to agricultural land and buildings are similar to those for business property. Subject to certain minimum ownership and use conditions, the two rates are again:

- 100 per cent for:
  - the person who owned the land farmed it themselves
  - agricultural property let for periods exceeding 12 months where letting commenced on or after 1 September 1995;
  - the land was used by someone else on a short-term grazing licence.
- 50 per cent for:
  - other qualifying property.

## Taper relief

A method of tapering relief applies where a donor dies within seven years of making a gift. It is not the gift, but the amount of tax, that is reduced. The Inheritance Tax is worked out at the rate prevailing as at the date of death and then reduced in accordance with the following table:

| Number of years between gift and death | % of tax rate on the gift |
|---|---|
| 3 to 4 | 32 |
| 4 to 5 | 24 |
| 5 to 6 | 16 |
| 6 to 7 | 8 |
| 7 or more | 0 |

The residence nil-rate band also tapers by £1 for every £2 more than the net value of an estate over £2 million.

---

Gavin Wood, a bachelor, made his nephew, Rhys, a cash gift of £350,000 on 4 May 2018. Gavin died in November 2024.

As Gavin did not survive for seven years, Rhys has to pay tax of £3,040 on his gift, calculated as follows:

|  | £ |
|---|---|
| Cash gift | 350,000 |
| *Less*: Gavin's annual exemption limits for 2016/17 and 2017/18 | 6,000 |
|  | 344,000 |
| *Less*: Nil rate band at the date of Gavin's death | 325,000 |
| Tax payable on | 19,000 |
| Inheritance Tax thereon @ 40 per cent | 7,600 |
| *Less*: Taper relief (60 per cent for surviving five years) | 4,560 |
| Tax payable | 3,040 |

---

It follows that there is no benefit of tapering relief where a PET, or the cumulative total of a number of PETs combined with any chargeable lifetime transfers, is within the limit of the nil rate band as at the date of death.

# Family home allowance

A family home allowance, which is worth £175,000, is added to the existing £325,000 nil rate band.

Known as the Residence Nil Rate Band (RNRB) it applies to the estate of an individual who:

- dies after 5 April 2017;
- owns a home, or a share in one, which is part of their estate;
- has a net estate not exceeding £2 million; and
- leaves the home, or a share of it, to their direct descendants.

A direct descendant of an individual is a child, grandchild or other lineal descendant, or a wife, husband or civil partner of a lineal descendant (incorporating their widower, widow or surviving civil partner).

For the purpose of this allowance a child is one who:

- has been their stepchild at any time;
- has been adopted;
- was fostered by them during their lifetime; or
- was under 18 when they were made a guardian or special guardian.

There are several other features of this allowance.

- If any part of the allowance is not used it can be transferred to the estate of the surviving spouse or partner. This rule still applies even if the first death was before 6 April 2017.
- For net estates worth more than £2 million, the allowance reduces by £1 for every £2 over this amount.
- It does not apply to lifetime gifts.
- It only applies to one home which the deceased must have lived in at some time.
- For house moves after 7 July 2015, and subject to certain conditions, it remains available to anyone who downsizes or ceases to own a home.

> Roy Fisher died on 19 July 2024. In his Will he left a home valued at £220,000 and other assets worth £110,000 to his three children. He was survived by his wife, Angela, who inherited the remainder of his estate.

|  | £ | £ |
|---|---|---|
| Value of assets left to children |  | 330,000 |
| Less: |  |  |
| Residence nil rate band | 175,000 |  |
| Basic nil rate band (part) | 155,000 | 330,000 |
| Taxable estate |  | Nil |

# Transferable nil rate band

Any part of the nil rate band not used on the first death of a married couple or civil partners is not lost. It is available to all survivors of a marriage or civil partnership.

It does not matter when the first spouse of a marriage died; it can have occurred at any time. However, for civil partnerships, the first death must be later than 4 December 2005 when the Civil Partnership Act came into effect.

Any amount of the unused nil rate band can only be transferred from one spouse to the surviving spouse when their relationship is ended by the death of one of them. In cases of divorce where one party to the broken marriage subsequently dies, the relief will not be available.

On the death of the survivor:

- the percentage limit of the nil rate band applying on the death of the first spouse or civil partner that was unused is applied to the nil rate band when the survivor dies; and
- the resulting amount is added to the survivor's own nil rate band.

Importantly, the transferable nil rate band and transferable RNRB must be claimed by executors within two years of the death.

---

Melvin Churchill died on 4 January 2010, leaving his estate of £200,000 to his wife, Eileen. She passed away on 10 December 2022, with an estate worth £600,000 divided between their four children.

When Melvin died, no part of the nil rate band at the time of £325,000 was used. Therefore, the nil rate band on Eileen's death is doubled to £650,000 and there is no Inheritance Tax to pay on her death.

> Janice Timms died on 21 July 1996. Her estate amounted to £400,000. In her Will she left £60,000 to each of her two children and the balance of her wealth to her husband, Colin. He passed away on 9 February 2023, having spent his last five years in a nursing home. His estate was worth £620,000 spread equally between the two children.
>
> When Janice died the nil rate band was £200,000, of which 60 per cent (£120,000) was used against the legacies to her two children, leaving 40 per cent to transfer to Colin on his death earlier this year. Colin's nil rate band of £325,000 is increased by 40 per cent to £455,000, leaving Inheritance Tax at 40 per cent payable on £165,000.

Someone who has lost more than one spouse or civil partner can bring forward all or part of any unused nil rate band on the estates of more than one of them. However, the total percentage of these unused nil rate bands is restricted to a maximum of 100 per cent between them.

> Marcia Bell died at home on 3 October 2024 leaving an estate valued at £850,000. She had been married twice, with both husbands passing away.
>
> Vernon's estate accounted for 40 per cent with 60 per cent left for Marcia.
>
> In working out the Inheritance Tax payable on Marcia's estate, which she left to her children, her executors can take into account the unused allowances brought forward from both marriages. However, she can only inherit a maximum of 100 per cent, giving a nil rate band of £650,000 on her death and with Inheritance Tax payable of £10,000 calculated as follows:
>
> |  | £ | £ |
> |---|---|---|
> | Value of Marcia's estate |  | 850,000 |
> | *Less*: |  |  |
> | Total of basic nil rate bands | 650,000 |  |
> | Residence nil rate band | 175,000 | 825,000 |
> | Tax payable on |  | 25,000 |
> | Inheritance Tax @ 40 per cent |  | 10,000 |

# Death

When someone dies, their assets pass into their estate to be administered by their personal representatives. Their main duties and responsibilities are to:

- gather in the assets of the deceased;
- settle their debts;
- pay out any legacies; and then
- distribute their remaining assets to the residuary beneficiaries.

It may also be necessary to complete a full Inheritance Tax Return and submit the form together with an application for a grant of:

- probate where there is a Will; or
- administration where there is no Will.

The Return must:

- be lodged within 12 months of the date of death; and
- include information about previous transfers and gifts in order that the amount of Inheritance Tax payable can be calculated.

In order to help your executors when the time comes, you are well advised to:

- let them know where your Will is kept;
- maintain up-to-date details of all your assets and where the supporting certificates and documents are stored; and
- keep complete records of your lifetime gifts.

---

Conrad Huxtable, a widower, died on 14 May 2024, leaving his entire estate to his son. He did not make any gifts in the seven years leading up to his death. His assets and unpaid bills at the time were:

| Assets | Value £ | £ |
|---|---|---|
| Home | 460,000 | |
| Household effects | 4,000 | |

*(continued)*

*(Continued)*

| Assets | Value £ | £ |
|---|---|---|
| Car | 3,000 | |
| Building society account | 20,000 | |
| National Savings | 8,000 | |
| Individual Savings Accounts | 13,000 | |
| Bank current account | 1,500 | |
| Outstanding State Pension | 540 | |
| Cash | 60 | |
| | | 510,100 |
| *Less:* | | |
| Allowable deductions | | |
| Funeral expenses | 1,410 | |
| Income tax | 620 | |
| Household bills | 440 | |
| Car repair | 230 | |
| | | 2,700 |
| Net value of estate | | 507,400 |
| *Less:* | | |
| Residence nil rate band | 175,000 | |
| Basic nil rate band | 325,000 | 500,000 |
| Tax payable on | | 7,400 |
| Inheritance Tax @ 40 per cent | | 2,960 |

\* When Conrad's wife died her entire nil rate band was used in working out the tax on her estate.

The tax is payable out of Conrad Huxtable's estate by the executors of his Will.

---

Joshua Winterbottom, a bachelor, who had lived in a nursing home for many years, died on 9 January 2021. He left an estate worth £620,000. Under his Will, Joshua bequeathed legacies totalling £40,000 to a number of charities with the balance of his estate to his nieces and nephews.

The Inheritance Tax payable by his executors is £91,800 as follows:

|  | £ | £ |
|---|---|---|
| Value of estate |  | 620,000 |
| Less: |  |  |
| Legacies to charities | 40,000 |  |
| Nil rate band | 325,000 | 365,000 |
| Tax payable on |  | 255,000 |
| Inheritance Tax @ 36 per cent |  | 91,800 |

The rate of Inheritance Tax is 36 per cent as the charitable legacies of £40,000 are more than 10 per cent of Joshua's estate after taking off the nil rate band (£620,000 – £325,000 = £295,000 x 10 per cent = £29,500).

Additionally, if a homeowner is going into care like in this scenario, they could potentially access downsizing relief. The downsizing relief rules simply mean that even where the deceased downsized to a less valuable home, or where they sold or gave away their home, an estate will potentially remain eligible for the proportion of the residence nil rate band that is foregone as a result of downsizing or selling the residence.

For help and advice on probate and Inheritance Tax following a death you can call HMRC on 0300 123 1072.

# Sales at a loss

Relief from Inheritance Tax is due on certain assets sold within specified time limits after death for less than their values at the date of death:

- for quoted securities the period is one year; and
- in the case of land and buildings, the time limit extends to four years.

The relief is available to the 'appropriate person', namely the person who pays the tax. All sales by that person in the respective periods must be aggregated. As a result, losses can be restricted or eliminated by profits so that the relief may be reduced or even lost. When this type of relief is claimed, the sale proceeds, before selling expenses, are substituted for the valuation at death. The Inheritance Tax liability is then reworked.

## Payment of tax

Primarily liable for the payment of Inheritance Tax are:

- the transferor in respect of chargeable lifetime gifts; and
- the personal representatives on death.

Personal representatives can draw on funds held in a deceased's bank and building society accounts solely for the purpose of paying any Inheritance Tax that is due before the Grant of Probate can be issued. The payment dates for Inheritance Tax are:

| Type of charge | Due date for payment |
| --- | --- |
| Chargeable lifetime gifts | Six months after the end of the month in which the gift was made |
| PETs that become taxable on death, and the charge on death | Six months after the end of the month in which death itself occurred |

There is an option to pay the tax due on some types of asset by 10 equal annual instalments. For lifetime transfers that are, or become, chargeable, this instalment option is only available if the tax is borne by the transferee. The first amount is, however, payable on the normal due date.

The assets concerned are:

- land and buildings;
- controlling shareholdings;
- unquoted shares, subject to certain conditions; and
- businesses.

Where the relevant asset is disposed of during the instalment paying period, all the outstanding instalments of Inheritance Tax become immediately payable.

## Interest and penalties

Interest is chargeable on Inheritance Tax liabilities from the due date until the date of payment. At the time of going to print, the rate of interest is

7.50 per cent. Any repayment of tax or interest thereon carries interest presently at the much lower rate of 4 per cent for the period from the date it was paid until it is refunded.

Where the instalment option is in effect, no interest is charged on the outstanding instalments of Inheritance Tax, except on:

- land and buildings that do not qualify for either business or agricultural property reliefs; and
- shares and securities in investment companies.

As with your Tax Return, there are penalties for late or incorrect Returns, delays, negligence or fraud as well as the late payment of Inheritance Tax.

## Excepted estates

Where no Inheritance Tax is due, the estate is usually referred to as an 'excepted estate' and a simpler form can be submitted as part of the probate process.

The estate will generally be an excepted estate if:

- the estate is worth £650,000 or less and any unused threshold is being transferred from a spouse or civil partner who died first; and
- it is classed as an exempt estate. This is where the deceased leaves everything to a spouse, civil partner or charity; or
- it is of low value; in other words under the threshold for Inheritance Tax – £325,000 for 2024/25; or
- the deceased was living permanently outside the UK (a foreign domiciliary) when they died and the value of their estate was £150,000 or less.

But, in some cases, a full Inheritance Tax Return may still be required even if there is no tax to pay depending on the assets and debts of an estate, and the history of lifetime giving.

## Intestacy

If you die without having made a Will, your estate will be distributed under the Intestate Estate Rules. There are two tables:

- one for an unmarried individual; and
- the other for a person with a surviving spouse.

| Unmarried individual | Division |
|---|---|
| Survived by:<br>    Children or grandchildren<br>    Parents<br>    Brothers and sisters<br>    Half-brothers and half-sisters<br>    Grandparents<br>    Uncles and aunts<br>    The Crown | The total estate is shared in the order of priority opposite, to the exclusion of all others |

| Married individual with surviving spouse | Division |
|---|---|
| (1) Estate amounts to less than £250,000 | All to spouse |
| (2) Estate exceeds £250,000 and there are children | Spouse is entitled to the personal belongings, the first £250,000 and half the remainder. The balance is shared between the children |
| (3) There are no children | All to spouse |

The spouse must survive the intestate individual by 28 days to become entitled under the intestacy rules.

Civil partners, and the children of a civil partnership, benefit under the intestacy rules in the same way as spouses and the children of a marriage.

It follows that if:

- you have a partner; but
- are not married,

he or she will not benefit from your estate under the intestacy rules. However, they will inherit any assets, including property, which you co-own jointly.

> **Tax Saver**
>
> On marriage any Will you have made is revoked. You must make a new Will otherwise the intestacy rules will determine who benefits, and by how much, from your estate.

## Legacies

If you are fortunate enough to receive a legacy from a member of your family or a friend, you should keep in mind the following.

- Any Inheritance Tax on a legacy will be accounted for by the executors before you receive it.
- You do not have to pay either Income Tax or Capital Gains Tax on a legacy.
- It does not need to be reported on your annual Tax Return.

## How to save on Inheritance Tax

> **Tax Saver**
>
> Here are some hints and tips on how to minimize the impact of Inheritance Tax on both your lifetime giving and the value of your estate on death.
>
> - First and foremost, make a Will. Otherwise your estate will devolve under the intestacy laws and maybe not in the way that you want. This is particularly relevant for co-habitees who have no entitlement where there is no Will.
> - Make sure you keep your Will up to date. Your finances and the value of your estate will change over time as will your personal circumstances and those of your family.
> - To make life as easy as possible for your executors, keep a file or register with up-to-date information of all your assets and where any certificates or documents are kept.
> - Maintain a record of your lifetime gifts.
> - Remember that gifts and transfers, during lifetime and on death, between husbands/wives and civil partners are exempt from Inheritance Tax.
> - Whenever you can afford to do so, make use of the various exemptions detailed in this chapter. By giving throughout your life you will significantly cut down on the amount of Inheritance Tax payable on your estate.

- The 'normal expenditure out of income' exemption is ideal for dealing with the payment of regular premiums on life policies written in Trust for younger generations. As the policy proceeds pass to them free of tax this is, in effect, a substitute for the payment of an Inheritance Tax liability on death, which cannot otherwise be avoided.
- Non-exempt gifts or transfers should be made as early as possible to increase your chances of surviving the seven-year period. Make immediately chargeable gifts – for example transfers into settlement – before those that are potentially exempt.
- Give assets that do not qualify for relief before those that do.
- If possible give assets with low values so that they appreciate in the hands of the recipient and outside your estate.
- Gifts and legacies to charities are exempt from Inheritance Tax. If you donate at least 10 per cent of your net estate to charity, the rate of Inheritance Tax payable on the balance comes down from 40 per cent to 36 per cent.
- Consider restricting the chargeable legacies for the next generations to an amount equivalent to the nil rate band for Inheritance Tax, leaving the remainder of your estate to your spouse or civil partner. He or she can then make gifts and hopefully live for a further seven years.
- In the two years after death, consider the use of a Deed of Variation in order to utilize any available exemptions that would otherwise be lost.

# 18
# Budget measures

In 2024 there were two major fiscal statements from the Chancellor – the first by Jeremy Hunt in March, and the second by Rachel Reeves in October.

However, it is important to note that 2024 was an election year with the Conservatives being replaced by a Labour government. This meant October 2024 featured the first Labour party budget in over 14 years.

Owing to the political differences in governments between these two speeches, the laws in place for 2024/25 naturally reflect the latter more. Therefore, we will focus on the Rachel Reeves statement in October (many of these points have already been touched upon in this book).

## Autumn Budget 2024

The main announcements in the Autumn Budget 2024 were as follows.

- Employer National Insurance Contributions increased from 13.8 per cent to 15 per cent from April 2025, whereupon the threshold above which employers pay these contributions will be reduced from £9,100 to £5,000 a year.
- At the same time, the Employment Allowance will increase from £5,000 to £10,500, and the £100,000 employer's National Insurance Contribution threshold for eligibility will be removed from 6 April 2025, increasing its availability to a larger number of employers.
- The main rates of Capital Gains Tax that apply to assets (other than residential property and carried interest) were increased from 10 per cent and 20 per cent to 18 per cent and 24 per cent, respectively. Similarly, the rate of Capital Gains Tax that applies on trustees and personal representatives was increased from 20 per cent to 24 per cent.
- The rate of Capital Gains Tax that applies to Business Asset Disposal Relief and Investors' Relief will increase from 10 per cent to 14 per cent from April 2025, and then again to 18 per cent from April 2026.

- Agricultural property relief and business property relief under Inheritance Tax is set to be reformed from April 2026, with 100 per cent relief for the first £1 million of combined assets and 50 per cent thereafter. Relief for shares not listed on a recognized stock exchange, such as AIM, will also be halved to 50 per cent from April 2026.

- The way company cars are taxed is being reformed with new rates for 2028/29 and 2029/30. This will mean Appropriate Percentages (APs) for zero-emission and electric vehicles will increase by 2 per cent per year, reaching an AP of 9 per cent in 2029/30. For cars with emissions of 1–50 g/km of $CO_2$, including hybrid vehicles, APs will rise to 18 per cent in 2028/29 and 19% in 2029/30. All other vehicle bands will see APs increase by 1 per cent per year, with the maximum AP reaching 39 per cent in 2029/30.

- The Stamp Duty Land Tax surcharge on second homes has increased to 5 per cent.

- Reform of 'non-dom' rules, with the status being replaced by a new residency-based test. By 2025 this will also bring foreign earnings into the Inheritance Tax system, though an extension period for people to bring their money and assets onshore has been increased from two years to three.

- Though no changes were made to Income Tax rates or allowances at the 2024 speech, the chancellor confirmed these will not be frozen beyond 2028.

- From April 2026, employers will be required to report and pay tax and Class 1A National Insurance Contributions on benefits-in-kind on a real time basis, with the exception of accommodation and loans. From this date, accommodation and loans may be payrolled on a voluntary basis, with mandatory payrolling to follow at a later date.

# APPENDICES

## 1. Flat-rate allowances for special clothing and the upkeep of tools for 2024/25

| (1) Fixed rate for all occupations | £ |
|---|---|
| Agricultural | 100 |
| Clothing | 60 |
| Forestry | 100 |
| Quarrying | 100 |
| Brass and copper | 120 |
| Precious metals | 100 |
| Food | 60 |
| Glass | 80 |
| Railways (non-craftspeople) | 100 |
| Uniformed prison officers | 80 |
| Uniformed bank and building society employees | 60 |
| Uniformed police officers up to and including Chief Inspector | 140 |
| Uniformed fire fighters and fire officers | 80 |

| (2) Variable rate depending on category of occupation | £ |
|---|---|
| Aircrew | |
| - pilots and co-pilots | 1,022 |
| - cabin crew | 720 |
| Forces Personnel | See Note (2) |
| Seamen | 140 to 165 |
| Iron mining | 100 to 120 |
| Iron and steel | 60 to 140 |

*(continued)*

*(Continued)*

| (2) Variable rate depending on category of occupation | £ |
|---|---|
| Aluminium | 60 to 140 |
| Engineering | 60 to 140 |
| Shipyards | 60 to 140 |
| Vehicles | 60 to 140 |
| Particular engineering | 60 to 140 |
| Constructional engineering | 60 to 140 |
| Electrical and electricity supply | 60 to 120 |
| Textiles and textile printing | 80 to 120 |
| Leather | 60 to 80 |
| Printing | 60 to 140 |
| Building materials | 60 to 120 |
| Wood and furniture | 60 to 140 |
| Building | 60 to 140 |
| Heating | 100 to 120 |
| Public service | 60 to 80 |
| Healthcare | 80 to 185 |

## *Notes*

**(1)** The allowances are only available to manual workers who have to bear the cost of upkeep of tools and special clothing. Other employees, such as office staff, cannot claim them.

**(2)** Forces Personnel can claim for the cost of laundering their uniform. The fixed annual allowance is £80 for the Royal Navy increasing to £100 for the RAF, Army and Royal Marines.

## 2. HMRC (VAT) notices and leaflets

| No | Title |
|---|---|
| 700 | The VAT Guide |
| 700/1 | Who should register for VAT? |
| 700/11 | Cancelling Your Registration |
| 700/12 | How to Fill in and Submit Your VAT Return |
| 700/18 | Relief from VAT on Bad Debts |
| 700/21 | Keeping VAT Records |
| 700/22 | Making Tax Digital for VAT |
| 700/41 | Late Registration Penalty |
| 700/42 | Misdeclaration and Repeated Misdeclaration Penalties |
| 700/43 | Default Interest |
| 700/45 | How to Correct VAT Errors and Make Adjustments or Claims |
| 700/50 | Default Surcharge |
| 700/58 | Treatment of VAT Repayment Returns and Supplements |
| 700/62 | Self Billing |
| 700/63 | Electronic Invoicing |
| 700/64 | Motoring Expenses |
| 700/65 | Business Entertainment |
| 706 | Partial Exemption |
| 727 | Retail Schemes |
| 731 | Cash Accounting |
| 732 | Annual Accounting |
| 733 | Flat Rate Scheme for Small Businesses |

# 3. Rates of National Insurance Contributions for 2024/25

**Class 1 Contributions for employers**

*Monthly threshold*

| | |
|---|---|
| Income of up to £9,100 | Nil |
| On income from £9,100 | 13.5% |

Note, this rate will rise to 15% from April 2025 and the threshold will lower to £5,000

**Class 1 Contributions for employees**

*Monthly income*

| | |
|---|---|
| On income up to £533 | Nil |
| On income between £533 and £1,048 | 8% |
| On income between £1,048 and £4,189 | 2% |
| Reduced rate for married women and widows with a valid election certificate on earnings below upper earnings limit | 1.85% |
| Rates for men and women over state pensionable age | Nil |

**Class 2 Voluntary contributions for the self-employed**

| | |
|---|---|
| Weekly flat rate | £3.45 |

**Class 3 Voluntary contributions**

| | |
|---|---|
| Weekly rate | £17.45 |

**Class 4 Contributions for the self-employed**

| | |
|---|---|
| On profits between £12,570 and £50,270 | 6% |
| On profits in excess of £50,270 | 2% |

# 4. Social Security benefits

## Taxable

Incapacity Benefit after the first 28 weeks (1) (2)
Employment and Support Allowance (contribution-based) (3)
Industrial Death Benefit Pensions
Jobseeker's Allowance
State Pension
Carer's Allowance (1)
Statutory Adoption Pay
Statutory Maternity and Paternity Pay
Statutory Shared Parental Pay
Statutory Sick Pay
Widowed Parent's and Bereavement Allowances

## Non-taxable

Incapacity Benefit for the first 28 weeks (1) (2)
Employment and Support Allowance (income-related) (3)
Income Support
Maternity Allowance
Child Benefit (4)
Child Tax Credit
Child Dependency Additions
Guardian's Allowance
Christmas Bonus for Pensioners
Industrial Injury Benefits
Disability Living Allowance
Personal Independence Payment (5)
Severe Disablement Allowance
Bereavement Payment (Lump Sum)
Universal Credit (6)
Housing Benefit
War Disablement Pensions

Social Fund Payments
Attendance Allowance
Vaccine Damage (Lump Sum)
Cold Weather and Winter Fuel Payments
Pension Credit
Working Tax Credit

## Notes

**(1)** Child dependency additions to these benefits are not taxable.

**(2)** Only paid to existing claimants on 27 October 2008.

**(3)** Replaced Incapacity Benefit for new claimants from 27 October 2008.

**(4)** Except for those liable to the High Income Tax Charge.

**(5)** Replaced Disability Living Allowance for new claimants from 8 April 2013.

**(6)** Has been introduced to replace previous benefits.

# 5. Rates of main Social Security benefits for 2024/25

| Weekly rate from April 2024 onwards | £ |
|---|---:|
| **Taxable** | |
| *New State Pension – retired after 5 April 2016* | 221.20 |
| *Old State Pension – retired before 6 April 2016* | |
| Single person | 169.50 |
| Married couples: both contributors – each | 169.50 |
| Wife not contributor – addition | 101.55 |
| Over 80s age addition (Old State Pension) | 0.25 |
| *Bereavement support* | |
| Higher rate – 1st payment | 3,500 |
| Higher rate – Monthly payment for 18 months | 350 |
| Lower rate – 1st payment | 2,500 |

*(continued)*

*(Continued)*

| | |
|---|---|
| Lower rate – Monthly payment for 18 months | 100 |
| *Employment and Support allowance* | |
| Age under 25 | 71.70 |
| Age 25 or over | 90.50 |
| *Jobseeker's allowance* | |
| Age under 25 | 71.70 |
| Age 25 or over | 90.50 |
| Couple both 18 or over | 142.25 |
| *Incapacity benefit* | |
| Long-term | 138.90 |
| Increase for age: | |
| • higher rate | 14.70 |
| • lower rate | 8.15 |
| Short-term (under pension age): | 104.85 |
| Short-term (over pension age): | 133.25 |
| *Statutory sick pay* | |
| Standard rate (weekly earnings threshold £120) | 116.75 |
| *Statutory maternity, paternity and adoption pay* | |
| Rate (weekly earnings threshold £120) | 184.03 |
| **Non-taxable** | |
| *Personal Independence Payment* | |
| Daily living component | |
| • enhanced rate | 108.55 |
| • standard rate | 72.65 |
| Mobility component | |
| • enhanced rate | 75.75 |
| • standard rate | 28.70 |
| **Maternity allowance** | |
| Standard rate | 184.03 |
| **Child benefit** | |
| Only or eldest child (couple or lone parent) | 25.60 |
| Each other child | 16.95 |

*(continued)*

*(Continued)*

| Weekly rate from April 2024 onwards | £ |
|---|---|
| **Attendance allowance** | |
| Higher rate | 108.55 |
| Lower rate | 72.65 |
| **Universal Credit*** | |
| Single under 25 | 311.68 |
| Single 25 or over | 393.45 |
| Joint claimant both under 25 | 489.23 |
| Joint claimant either 25 or over | 617.60 |

*Monthly rates.

# 6. HMRC (Revenue) explanatory booklets, leaflets and helpsheets

## Booklets and leaflets

| No | Title |
|---|---|
| IR 115 | Paying for Childcare: Getting help from your employer |
| 480 | Expenses and Benefits: A tax guide |
| 490 | Employee Travel – A Tax and NIC's Guide |
| SE 1 | Setting Up in Business |
| SE 2 | Giving your business the best start with tax |
| RK BK 1 | Keeping Records for Your Tax Return |
| HMRC 1 | HMRC Decisions: What to do if you disagree |
| RDR 1 | Residence, domicile and the remittance basis |
| WTC 2 | Child Tax Credit and Working Tax Credit: A guide |
| WTC 5 | Working Tax Credit – help with the costs of childcare |
| WTC5/CP | Working Tax Credit – Childcare element |
| WTC 7 | Tax Credit Penalties |

# Helpsheets

## General

| | |
|---|---|
| HS204 | Limit on Income Tax reliefs |
| HS223 | Rent-a-Room scheme |
| HS253 | Furnished holiday lettings |
| HS305 | Employment-related shares and securities |
| HS320 | Gains on UK Life Assurance policies |
| HS325 | Other Taxable Income |
| HS341 | Enterprise Investment Scheme: Income Tax relief |
| HS342 | Charitable Giving |
| H343 | Accrued Income Scheme |

## Employment

| | |
|---|---|
| HS201 | Vouchers, Credit Cards and Tokens |
| HS202 | Living Accommodation |
| HS203 | Car Benefits and Car Fuel Benefits |
| HS207 | Non-Taxable Payments or Benefits for Employees |
| HS208 | Payslips and Coding Notices |
| HS210 | Assets Provided for Private Use |
| HS211 | Employment: Residence and domicile issues |

## Self-employment

| | |
|---|---|
| HS220 | More than One Business |
| HS222 | How to Calculate Your Taxable Profits |
| HS227 | Losses |
| HS229 | Information from Your Accounts |
| HS252 | Capital Allowances and Balancing Charges |

# 7. Main dates of the Self Assessment calendar: Saturday 6 April 2024 to Saturday 5 April 2025

| Date | What happens | Who is affected |
|---|---|---|
| 6 April 2024 | 2023/24 Tax Returns sent out by HMRC. | Taxpayers who need to fill in an annual Tax Return. |
| 1 May 2024 | Daily penalty of £10, up to a maximum of £900. | Taxpayers who have failed to complete their 2022/23 Tax Return. |
| 31 July 2024 | Second payment on account due for 2023/24. | Those taxpayers who make regular half-yearly payments on account. |
| 1 August 2024 | First tax geared penalty levied for failing to submit a 2022/23 Tax Return before this date. | Taxpayers who have not yet completed and sent back their 2022/23 Tax Returns. |
| 3 August 2024 | Further 5 per cent late payment penalty on tax still outstanding for 2023/24. | Late payers of tax still due for 2022/23. |
| 31 October 2024 | Filing deadline for completing and returning 2023/24 paper Tax Returns. | Taxpayers who want HMRC to: calculate their tax for 2023/24; and collect tax owing for 2023/24 of less than £3,000 through their code number in 2025/26. |
| 31 December 2024 | Non-mandatory filing deadline for 2023/24 online Tax Returns. | Online filers who want HMRC to collect tax owing for 2023/24 of less than £3,000 through their code number in 2025/26. |
| 31 January 2025 | Filing deadline for 2023/24 online Tax Returns. Payment date for the balance of tax due for 2022/23 and the first payment on account for 2023/24. | Taxpayers sent a 2022/23 Tax Return. Taxpayers who need to settle either of these liabilities. |
| 1 February 2025 | First penalty notices issued for the late filing of a 2022/23 Tax Return. | Taxpayers who were sent a 2023/24 Tax Return. |
| 3 March 2025 | First 5 per cent late payment penalty imposed for failing to pay tax due by 31 January 2025 and still outstanding on 3 March 2025. | Late payers of tax for 2023/24. |

# INDEX

accounting 79–82, 118
    annual 71–72, 74
    cash 70–71, 83, 202
accounts offices 4–5, 194–95
accruals-based accounting 79, 80, 118
additional information pages (Tax Returns) 81, 170, 174, 181, 188
additional rate (45% rate) tax 11, 31, 116, 117, 122, 168, 189
adjudicators 9
agricultural property relief 205, 210, 224
annual accounting 71–72, 74, 82
annual pension contributions 109–10
annuities 27, 28, 111, 146, 173
appeals
    Income Tax 7, 8, 196, 197, 199
    VAT 75
apportionment 67, 80–81, 147, 154, 159, 160, 164
appropriate percentages 50, 224
Approved Profit Sharing Schemes 56
arrivers 142, 143
assessments 8
    *see also* Self Assessment
assets
    owned on 31 March 1982 158
    part disposal of 164
    pre-owned 206–07, 209
Attendance Allowance 102, 104, 232
automatic residence test 142
Autumn Budgets (Statements) 9
    Autumn Budget (2024) 52, 60, 93, 119, 149, 152, 223–24

back-dating VAT claims 67
BACS payments 195
bad debts 68–69, 202
bank accounts 78
Bank Giro payments 195
basic (20%) tax rate 11, 13, 116, 117
beneficial loans 54
benefits cap 103–04
benefits-in-kind 38–39, 49–54, 58, 224
bereavement support 230–31
bicycles 46, 47, 59
BIK rates 51–52
blind person's allowance 12, 13, 19, 37, 179, 201
bonds 118, 121, 122–24

BR tax code 40
Budget Payment Plan 193
Budget Statements 9
    Autumn Budget (2024) 52, 60, 93, 119, 149, 152, 223–24
business acquisitions 61
Business Asset Disposal Relief 156–57, 204, 223
business loans 30
business mileage 52
Business Payment Support Service 194
business property 205, 209–10
business travel 45, 46, 47–48, 144, 175
buy-to-let income 27, 28–29, 152, 184, 185

C tax code 39
cap on state benefits 103–04
capital 103
capital allowances 88, 119, 202
capital gains 89, 151, 173, 204
capital gains exemptions 151
Capital Gains Tax (CGT) 1, 31–33, 55–57, 131, 146–48, 151–66, 168, 189, 196, 223
Capital Gains Tax (CGT) deferral 165
capital introduced 79
capital limits (state benefits) 102–03
carbon dioxide ($CO_2$) emissions 50–52, 53, 68, 224
Carer's Allowance 99, 104
'carried back' donations 32
cars 67–68
    *see also* company cars; electric vehicles; lease cars; pooled vehicles; private car usage
cash accounting 70–71, 79, 80, 83, 202
cash books 78
Chancellor of the Exchequer 9, 223
change in circumstances notification 25–26, 37
CHAPS payments 195
chargeable gains calculation 154–55
chargeable lifetime transfers 206, 218
charitable bequests 32–33, 206, 209, 222
chattels 162–63
cheque payments 193
Child Benefit 99, 101–02, 133, 167, 180, *181*, 231
child element rate (Child Tax Credit) 22

# Index

Child Support Agency  136
Child Tax Credit  21–22, 133
Child Trust Fund  134–35
childcare  46, 134
childcare element (Working Tax Credit)  23
children  132–33, 212
Citizens Advice Bureau  26, 112
Civil Partnership Act (2005)  213
civil partnerships  16, 131, 136, 146, 153–54, 162, 201, 207, 213–14, 220
Class 1 NICs  96–97, 99, 224, 228
Class 2 NICs  96, 97, 228
Class 3 NICs  96, 98, 228
Class 4 NICs  96, 98, 228
close companies  27
closure notices  7
clothing expenses  45, 225
Code of Practice (No 1) (HMRC)  195
Coding Notices (PAYE)  36–41, 137, 196
Collector of Taxes  91
company cars  38, 50–52, 68, 224
company directors  49, 56, 127, 167
company shares  30
company vans  53
complaints  8–9, 75
compliance checks  6–7
computer equipment  46, 49, 62, 82, 86
contracts  77
Corporation Tax  88, 93
Court Orders  135, 136
Covid-19  48

D tax code  40
death
    pension benefits  112–13
    and personal allowances  138–39
debt (bad debts)  68–69, 202
Deeds of Variation  132, 222
defined contribution pensions  112
Department for Work and Pensions (DWP)  98, 99, 108, 172
diesel cars  50
Direct Debit
    tax payments  192–93
    VAT payments  66
directors  49, 56, 127, 167
disability
    benefits  22, 23, 99, 102, 104, 108, 134, 229
    tax relief  46, 47, 52, 160, 206
Disability Living Allowance  102, 104
disabled child element (Child Tax Credit)  22, 23
discretionary trusts  132
dividend income  55, 117, 128, 146, 168, 173, 175, 184, 185, 186
divorce  135–36, 213

domicile status  141, 148–49, 219, 232, 233
Double Taxation Agreement  145, 146
drawdowns, pension  111–12
drawings  79
DWP (Department for Work and Pensions)  98, 99, 108, 172

earnings  36
education  60
electric vehicles  46, 50, 224
emergency tax codes  40
employed status  3, 35–58, 172, 233
employee share ownership  55–57
employee shareholders  57
'employees with areas' travel  48
Employer National Insurance Contributions  223, 228
employer registration  91
Employment and Support Allowance  24, 223, 229, 231
Enterprise Investment Scheme  127, 164–65, 203
Enterprise Management Incentives  57
estate administration  215–17
European Union (EU)  64, 93
excepted estates  219
executors  213, 215, 221
exempt estates  219
Extra-Statutory Concessions  9
eye tests  45

family element (Child Tax Credit)  22
family home allowance  211–13
farming sector  94
    see also agricultural property relief
filing deadlines  169–70, 183, 187, 190, 197–98
Finance Act (2003)  154
Finance Acts (Bills)  9, 154
5% VAT rate  59
fixed costs  80
Fixed-Interest Savings Certificates  115
fixed-rate deduction scheme  83–84, 119
fixed-rate investments  118
Flat Rate Scheme  66, 69–70
foreign domicile status  219
foreign income and gains  149
40% (higher) tax rate  11, 14, 31, 33, 116–17, 121–22, 178, 189
45% (additional) rate  11, 31, 116, 117, 122, 168, 189
foster carers  92–93
free shares  55
fuel benefits  53
fuel scale charges  67–68
full expensing  88
furnished holiday accommodation  93–94

# Index

Furnished Holiday Let regime 119

Gift Aid 30–32, 178–79, 202
'gift with reservation' 206–07, 209
gifts 32–33, 45, 132, 151, 156, 163, 206–09, 215, 222
gifts of assets to charities 32–33
Government Gateway accounts 6
Grant of Probate 215, 218

health checks 45
Help-to-Save Scheme 126–27
helpline numbers
    HMRC 4, 171, 194
    Inheritance Tax 205, 217
    National Advice Service (VAT) 59
    National Insurance Registrations 95
    Pension Service 109, 175
    Tax Credits 26
High Income Child Benefit charge 133, 180, *181*
High Net Worth Units 4
higher (40%) tax rate 11, 14, 31, 33, 116, 117, 121–22, 178, 189
HMRC (HM Revenue & Customs)
    accounts offices 4–5, 194–95
    address 5
    adjudicators 9
    booklets/ helpsheets 227, 232–34
    Code of Practice (No 1) 195
    complaint handling 8–9
    determinations 7
    enquiry handling 6–7
    Form CA72A 97
    Form CG34 163
    Form 18 17
    Form P9D 172
    Form P11D 49, 172, 175
    Form P45 43–44, 172, 174, 175
    Form P50Z 112
    Form P53 112
    Form P55 112
    Form P60 41–43, 172, 174, 175
    Form P85 144
    Form P160 172
    Form P161 137
    Form R43 145
    Form 17 128
    Form VAT1 61
    National Insurance Contributions and Employer Office 97
    new starter checklist 43
    online services 61, 65–66, 71, 78, 109, 168–69, 192, 197
    tax offices 3–4
    tax registration service 78

holiday accommodation 93–94, 119
home annuity loans 28
home ownership 145–48, 204
    and inheritance tax 209, 211
    sale (purchase) of 154–55, 159–62, 224
home-to-work travel 47, 52, 53
home working 46, 48–49, 80, 83–84
household expenses 49
Hunt, Jeremy 223
hybrid vehicles 50

Incapacity Benefit 231
incidental expenses 46, 155
income, accrued 79, 80, 118
income disregard 26
income splitting 128–29, 131
Income Tax 1, 11–13, 36, 39, 54–55, 57, 92–93, 141, 190, 224
    *see also* tax relief
independent school VAT 60
Index-Linked Savings Certificates 115
Individual Savings Accounts (ISAs) 116, 124–26, 134, 135, 151
Inheritance Tax 1, 112, 132, 166, 205–22, 224
Inheritance Tax calculation 215–17
Inheritance Tax exemptions 207–09, 221–22
Inheritance Tax Office 205
Inheritance Tax payment 218
Inheritance Tax Returns 215
Inheritance Tax threshold 205
Inland Revenue Approved Share Option Plans 56–57
input tax 64, 65, 66–68, 70
insurance 45, 54, 58
    life insurance policies 121–24
interest charges
    Income Tax 195, 197–99
    Inheritance Tax 218–19
    VAT late payment 74, 202
interest-free loans 54
interest payments 27
interim VAT payments 71
intestacy 219–20, 221
investment income 115–29, 168, 173, 189, 203
    *see also* open-ended investment companies; Seed Enterprise Investment Scheme (SEIS)
Investors' Relief 157–58, 223
ISAs 116, 124–26, 134, 135, 151

Jobcentre Plus 44, 98
JobSeeker's Allowance 24, 231
joint income 128–29, 131

# Index

joint tenancy between spouses (civil partners) 209
jointly owned assets 146, 154, 203
Junior Individual Savings Account 134, 135

K tax code 40, 137

L tax code 39
late-night journeys home 46, 52
late payments (interest charges)
  income tax 195, 196, 197–99
  Inheritance Tax 218–19
  VAT 68–69, 74, 202
lease cars 67
leases of land 164
leavers 142, 143
legacies 221, 222
legislation 9
letting (rental) income 28–29, 118–20, 121, 145–46, 173, 185, 189, 233
  *see also* buy-to-let income
life annuities 27
life insurance policies 121–24
lifetime gifts 209, 215
Lifetime ISAs 126
limited company status 92
living accommodation 54
living together 131
Lloyds Underwriters 94
loans 27, 54
long service awards 45
losses 83, 88–90, 155–56, 173, 202–03, 217–18

M tax code 39
machinery (plant) purchases 27, 30, 91, 210
maintenance payments 136, 181
marital separation 135–36, 154
marriage 131, 146, 153–54, 208
Marriage Allowance 12, 13, 14–15, 37, 136, 180, 201
Married Couples Allowance *12*, 14–19, 131, 135, 136, 139, 182, 201, 230
matching shares 55
Maternity Allowance 231
Maternity Pay 99, 231
medical insurance 54, 58
medical treatment 45
Members of Parliament 9
micro-entrepreneurs 84
mileage allowances 46–47, 52, 53, 184
mobile telephones 46
mortgages 28, 29, 80, 82, 151
moving jobs 43–44
multiple workplace business travel 48

N tax code 39
National Advice Service 59
National Insurance Contributions 1, 4, 36, 55, 95–98, 102, 107, 108, 223, 228
National Insurance Contributions and Employer Office 97
National Insurance Contributions deferment 97
National Insurance numbers (NINOs) 6, *38*, 95, 148, 169, 191
National Insurance Records 98, 107, 108
National Savings and Investments 115, 134, 151
new businesses 89
new starter checklist (HMRC) 43
nil-band tax rate 152, 205, 211, 213–14, 222
nominal value 118
non-domiciliaries ('non-doms') 149, 224
non-qualifying life insurance policies 121–24
non-taxable social security benefits 229–30
  *see also* Attendance Allowance; Child Benefit; Child Tax Credit; Maternity Allowance; Personal Independent Payments; Universal Credit
non-UK resident allowances 144–48
'normal expenditure out of income' exemption 222
Notice of Coding (PAYE Coding Notices) 36–41, 137, 196
NT tax code 40

office equipment 46, 49, 62
Officer in Charge 8
Ombudsman 9
1257L tax code 40
online services 61, 65–66, 71, 78, 109, 168–69, 192, 197
open-ended investment companies 125, 158
OT tax code 39
out-placement counselling 45
output tax 64, *65*
overseas employment 46, 58, 144, 148
overseas investment income 128, 141, 175
overseas residence test 142

paper Tax Return deadline 197
Parental Leave (Pay) 100
parking facilities 46
Parliamentary and Health Service Ombudsman 9
part disposal of assets 164
part surrender of non-qualifying life policies 122
partnership shares 55

# Index

partnerships 27, 30, 91
Paternity Pay 99–100, 231
Pay As You Earn (PAYE) 3, 36, 167, 189–90
PAYE Coding Notices 36–41, 137, 196
payment dates 189–90
payment in lieu of notice 58
Payment Support Service 194
payments on account 190–91
payroll giving 33
P11D 49, 172, 175
penalties (late payment)
    income tax 195, 196, 197–99
    Inheritance Tax 218–19
    VAT 68–69, 74, 202
penalty notices 196
pension contributions (private pensions) 109–10
Pension Credit 24, 104–05
Pension Direct Service 175
Pension, Disability and Carers Service 98
pension drawdowns 111–12
pension input period 110
Pension Service 109
Pension Wise 112
pensioners 98, 136–38, 168
    *see also* retirement
pensions 3, 45, 172, 175, 177–78
    private 109–13
    State Pension 40, 102, 107–09, 137, 175, 230
permanent job moves to United Kingdom moves 148
permanent workplace status 48
personal allowances 12, 13–14, 37, 39, 131, 132, 173, 201
Personal Independence Payments (PIP) 102, 104, 231
Personal Savings Allowance 116
Personal Tax Accounts 6, 192
petty cash books 78
P45 43–44, 172, 174, 175
plant (machinery) purchases 27, 30, 91, 210
political party gifting 209
pooled vehicles 53
post-cessation expenses 87–88, 202
post-employment notice pay 58
postal tax payments 193, 195
potentially exempt transfers (PETs) 206, 211, 218
pre-owned assets 206–07, 209
pre-trading expenses 87
Premium Bond Prizes 115
private car usage 44, 49, 52, 80–81, 83
'private pension schemes' 109–13
private school VAT 60

probate 215, 218
professional body subscriptions 44, 49, 175
profit sharing schemes 56
profits for tax 86–87
prosecutions 8
P60 41–43, 172, 174, 175

'qualifying' political party gifting 209

'reasonable' late tax filing excuses 197–98
record-keeping 171–74, 198, 215, 221
    self-employment 78–79, 83
reduced payments on account 190–91
reduced VAT rate 59
redundancy payments 58, 96
Reeves, Rachel 223
refunds (repayments) 65, 171, 192
regular gifts 208
relocation expenses 54
remission of tax 196
rent-a-room relief 120–21, 203
rental expenses 119, 120
rental (letting) income 28–29, 118–20, 121, 145–46, 173, 185, 189, 233
    *see also* buy-to-let income
replacement loans 27
residence 141–48
Residence Nil Rate Band 211–13
residence test 142
residential property (home ownership) 145–48, 204
    and inheritance tax 209, 211
    sale (purchase) of 154–55, 159–62, 224
retail sector 69
retirement 92, 107, 137–38
    *see also* pensioners; pensions
retraining courses 45
Royal Assent 9

S tax code 39
sales at a loss 217–18
savings income 115–29, 168, 203
    *see also* ISAs
Savings-Related Share Option Schemes 56
Scottish Income Tax 11–12
second home ownership 161–62, 224
Seed Enterprise Investment Scheme (SEIS) 127–28, 165, 181, 203
SEF1 (Tax Return) 202
Self Assessment
    calendar 234
    registration 168–69
    *see also* Tax Returns

Self Assessment Unique Taxpayer
    References 5
self-billing 64
self-employment 3, 5, 77–94, 109, 167, 190,
    202–03, 228, 233
  see also Self Assessment
service engineers 48
severely disabled child element (Child Tax
    Credit) 22, 23
Share Incentive Plans 55–56
Share Option Plans 56–57
Shared Parental Leave (Pay) 100
shareholders 57
shares 27, 30, 32–33, 151, 156, 158–59,
    168, 204, 210, 224
  employee share ownership 55–57
  free 55
short life assets 163–64
Sick Pay 99, 231
single premium life insurance policies
    121–24
site-based workers 47
small business income allowance 84, 202
small businesses 69–70, 84, 90–91, 202
small property income allowance 203
social security (state) benefits 1, 98–105,
    229–32
  see also blind person's allowance; Child
    Benefit; State Pension
spouses 91, 125, 131, 162, 207,
    213–14, 220
  see also marriage; Marriage Allowance;
    Married Couples Allowance
staff canteens 45
staff parties 45
Stamp Duty Land Tax 160–61, 224
Stamp Duty Reserve Tax 158
standard VAT rate 59, 60, 69
State Pension 40, 102, 107–09, 137,
    175, 230
State Pension Age 96, 101
State Pension claim process 108
State Pension Credit 24, 104–05
State Pension deferment 108
State Pension forecasts 108–09
State Pension qualifying years 107
Statements of Account 191–92
Statements of Practice 9
Statutory Maternity Pay 99, 231
Statutory Paternity Pay 99–100, 231
Statutory Sick Pay 99, 231
stocks 115, 116, 118, 124–25, 135
subcontractors 94
sufficient ties test 141, 142–43

supplementary self-employment pages
    84–86, 170, 171, 183
Supreme Court 8

T tax code 39
tangible moveable property 164
taper relief 210–11
tax advisers 7
Tax Calculation Summary 182
tax calculations 183–87
tax codes (PAYE Coding Notices) 36–41,
    137, 196
Tax Credit Office 22
tax credit renewals 24–25
tax credits 1, 21–26, 29, 201
Tax-Free Childcare 134
tax inspectors 8
tax offices 3–4, 8–9
tax payment date of receipt 194–95
tax payment due dates 189–90
tax payment difficulties 194
tax payments 39, 189–99
  see also late payments (interest charges)
tax rates 11–12
  additional (45%) 31, 116, 117, 122,
    168, 189
  basic (20%) 13, 116, 117
  nil-rate 152, 205, 211, 213–14, 222
tax refunds 171, 192
tax registration service 78
tax relief 27–33, 44–47, 155–58
  agricultural property 205, 210, 224
  Business Asset Disposal Relief 204, 223
  caps 90–91
  Enterprise Investment Scheme 127
  Inheritance tax 217–18
  losses 88–90
  pension contributions 109–10
  rent-a-room 120–21, 203
  Seed Enterprise Investment Scheme
    127–28
tax remission 196
Tax Return amendments 188
Tax Return declaration 183
Tax Return format 170
Tax Return signatures 188
Tax Returns 3, 5, 6–7, 79, 83, 84–86,
    167–88
  additional information pages 81
  filing deadlines 190, 197–98
  SEF1 202
  see also tax payments
tax underpayments 39
tax year 79

# Index

taxable profit 86–87
taxable social security benefits 229
    *see also* Carer's Allowance; State Pension; Statutory Maternity Pay; Statutory Paternity Pay; Statutory Sick Pay
taxi fares 46
Temporary Repatriation Facility 149
tenancy in common 209
terminal loss offsetting 89–90
termination of employment payments 58
tools allowances 45, 226
'top slicing' relief 123–24
TR2 (Tax Return) 171
TR3 (Tax Return) 175, 177
TR4 (Tax Return) 177, 179
TR5 (Tax Return) 179–80
TR6 (Tax Return) 182–83
TR7 (Tax Return) 188
TR8 (Tax Returns) 183
training 45, 60
transferable marriage allowance 12, 13, 14–15, 37, 136, 201
transferable nil-rate tax band 213–14
travel 45, 46, 47–48, 144, 175
    home-to-work 52, 53
    *see also* business travel
trivial benefits-in-kind 49
trusts 132
    *see also* Venture Capital Trusts (VCTs)
20% tax rate 11, 13, 116, 117

UK residence test 142
uncrystallized funds 111
underpayment collection 39
unincorporated businesses 79, 210
Unique Taxpayer Reference (UTR) 5, 169
Universal Credit 21, 98, 100–01, 133, 232
unused pension contributions allowances 110–11

valuations 163
VAT (Value Added Tax) 1, 59
    annual accounting 71–72
    appeals 75
    cash accounting 70–71
    complaints 75
    de-registration 63
    error disclosures 73
    exemptions 60
    flat rate scheme 69–70
    input tax 66–67
    inspections 72
    invoices 63–64
    late payment of 68–69, 72–74, 202
    motor vehicles (fuel) 67–68
    rates 59–60
    registration 60–63, 66, 202
    repayments 65
    retail sector 69
    VAT Returns (VAT100) 64–66, 69
VAT, Customs and Excise Helpline 63
'VAT fraction' 69
VAT officers 75
VAT payable calculation 64
VAT registration certificates 61
VAT registration number 61, 62, 66
VAT1 61
VAT 100 64–66, 69
Venture Capital Trusts (VCTs) 116, 128, 151, 165–66
Voluntary National Insurance Contributions 98, 107, 228
voluntary VAT registration 62

wasting assets 163–64
wedding gifts 208
'wholly disproportionate' threshold 122
widowed status 108, 139
Wills 215, 220, 221
working abroad (overseas employment) 46, 58, 144, 148
working from home (home working) 46, 48–49, 80, 83–84
Working Tax Credit (WTC) 21, 23, 24

X tax code 40

zero-rated VAT 60

## Looking for another book?

Explore our award-winning books from global business experts in General Business

Scan the code to browse

www.koganpage.com/general-business